Learning About Punctuation

Learning About Punctuation

Edited by
Nigel Hall and Anne Robinson

Heinemann
Portsmouth, NH

Heinemann
A Division of Reed Elsevier Inc.
361 Hanover Street
Portsmouth, NH 03801-3912

Offices and agents throughout the world

Library of Congress Cataloging in Publication Data

Learning About Punctuation/Edited by Nigel Hall and Anne Robinson
The Language and Education Library: 9
Includes bibliographical references and index
1. English language–Punctuation–Study and teaching.
I. Hall, Nigel, 1947-   . II. Robinson, Anne III. Series.
PE1450.L37   1996
428'.007–dc20   95-40871

ISBN 0-435-07209-9

Published simultaneously in the United States in 1996 by Heinemann and in the rest of the world by Multilingual Matters Ltd, Frankfurt Lodge, Clevedon Hall, Victoria Road, Clevedon, Avon BS21 7SJ, UK.

Printed and bound in Great Britain by WBC Book Manufacturers Ltd.

Contents

Contributors

Holly Anderson is Senior Lecturer at Homerton College, Cambridge, UK.

Candice Arthur is a Research Student on the Punctuation Project at Manchester Metropolitan University, UK.

Yetta Goodman is Professor of Education at the University of Arizona, Tucson, Arizona, USA.

Nigel Hall is Reader in Literacy Education in the Didsbury School of Education at Manchester Metropolitan University, Manchester, UK.

Ros Ivanic is a Lecturer in the Department of Linguistics at Lancaster University, Lancaster, UK.

Prisca Martens is an Associate Professor at Indiana University, Indianapolis, USA.

Katharine Perera is Professor of Educational Linguistics at Manchester University, Manchester, UK.

Anne Robinson is Senior Lecturer in the Didsbury School of Education at Manchester Metropolitan University, Manchester, UK.

Nadeen Ruiz is Associate Professor in the Bilingual Multicultural Education Department at the California State University, Sacramento, California, USA.

Sandra Wilde is an Assistant Professor at the University of Oregon, Oregon, USA.

Introduction

It is now four years since we were approached by a number of school headteachers (principals) who were worried about punctuation. As will be clearer from Chapter 5 in this book, British teachers of younger children were not particularly concerned about punctuation. Their emphasis was on encouraging children to be makers of meaning rather than analysts of structure. Punctuation was something that could be taken care of later when the children were more experienced and confident writers. All this changed when the British Government introduced a National Curriculum which demanded that children by the age of seven had to achieve certain competencies with punctuation which had never been expected before. Hence the new concerns of the headteachers.

We began to seek for some answers which would help these teachers. One of our first acts was to begin an extended search for everything written and researched on the topic of learning and teaching punctuation. At this point we made what seemed to us a bizarre discovery. Although punctuation as a topic had received quite a bit of attention from linguists, historians, students of literacy style etc. there was hardly any research examining how young children came to understand the notion of punctuation. We expanded our search, exploiting many personal contacts across the world, but eventually had to face up to the fact that our initial survey was correct. Very little research literature existed which could help professionals understand how beginning readers and writers came to make sense of punctuation. Thus, all the claims in articles about teaching punctuation and the demands of the British National Curriculum documents were predicated upon virtually no research evidence.

As a consequence of our initial work we set up 'The Punctuation Project' in the UK. This is a generic title for a number of projects which are currently being undertaken. All of these are of recent origin so only two have reports in this book. These projects are examining a number of interesting questions about the learning and teaching of punctuation.

Our search also revealed, not surprisingly, that there was no book which pulled together what had been researched about punctuation in a way that

1

might help teachers. It was with this in mind that we decided to try and put together a first ever book devoted to learning about punctuation. We have tried to assemble in this book papers by those people we have been able to trace who have, in recent years, undertaken, or are currently undertaking, investigations into some aspect of learning about punctuation. It is not a complete collection; for various reasons a couple of important contributions were unable to be included in this book. Nevertheless, we hope that what is here is sufficient to interest people in the topic.

Anyone writing about punctuation steps into a minefield and we fully expect people to find all kinds of problems with our own punctuation. We are not making the claim to know everything about how to punctuate; our interest is in how beginning readers and writers grow to understand punctuation. We have, for the most part, expected authors to be responsible for the punctuation of their chapters. If they have differences from each other then that simply reflects the stylistic licence of punctuation and, in some cases, cultural differences.

Readers from outside the UK will find (as in this introduction) some references to the British National Curriculum. Please do not be put off by this. Wherever references occur we have made sure that there is sufficient information available to explain them. In most cases, mention of the National Curriculum is simply a backdrop to introducing wider questions about the learning of punctuation. One other cultural point needs mention and the word 'point' is the precise one. British and North American punctuation styles are largely similar, although there are some differences. One minor one is that in the US the word 'period' is used where in the UK we use the term 'full stop'. Somewhat paradoxically it seems that it is the British reference which has changed as the word 'period' was prevalent in Britain long before 'full stop'. In this book we have tended to leave authors to use whatever term is normal for them. Readers from outside the UK will have to accept British punctuation through most of this book. Anyone interested in the differences between North American and British punctuation should read 'You have a point there' by Eric Partridge. Although a book about British punctuation, it has a chapter about the differences to be found in North American punctuation.

Although the book is not divided into sections, the chapters can be grouped in clusters. The first is a cluster of one as Nigel Hall offers a substantial overview and review of some of the issues and research pertaining to the understanding of punctuation by beginning readers and writers.

Then follows a cluster of three chapters which have their main focus (but not exclusively) in the classroom use of writing by young children. In Chapter 2, Yetta Goodman and Prisca Martens look at the inventive quality of young children's punctuation and how this reflects the considerable intellectual qualities of younger writers. In Chapter 3, Holly Anderson looks at one seven-year-old child who seems particularly able to reflect explicitly on her use of punctuation. In Chapter 4, Sandra Wilde explores the development of a group of slightly older American children as they move from Grade 3 to Grade 4 in an American school.

The next cluster features two chapters which focus on teachers. In Chapter 5, Anne Robinson reports on interviews with a range of teachers about their own experiences with punctuation, their beliefs about how it should be taught and their judgements on what they are being asked to achieve by Britain's National Curriculum. In Chapter 6, Candice Arthur examines one short lesson which was, among other things, meant to help a group of six-year-olds learn something about punctuation. She shows that explaining punctuation is hardly a straightforward affair where young children are concerned.

The final cluster is of three chapters which represent more intense studies of particular areas of punctuation knowledge and development. In Chapter 7, Nadeen Ruiz offers a fascinating account of how a young deaf child developed skills in punctuation. Her chapter invites teachers of younger children to examine this deaf child's ability to make sense of what many see as a very oral task and reflect upon their own teaching of punctuation. In Chapter 8, Katharine Perera offers a rare study of punctuation and reading. She looks closely at how young children are influenced by the punctuation of speech as they read. Finally, in Chapter 9, Ros Ivanic reminds us that it is not only children who face the complexities of learning about punctuation. She describes a study carried out with adult basic writers and explores the ways in which they tried to make sense of the object called punctuation. It is salutary for teachers to reflect on the beliefs of these adults and ask whether their current teaching practices are likely to prevent such confusion in the future.

This is not a book about how to teach punctuation although clearly many of the chapters have implications for how teachers should proceed. There are many views about how punctuation should be taught, but we believe that the primary concern at the moment is to understand more about how beginning learners make sense of a complex issue like punctuation. We have too many views and not enough evidence. This book is an attempt to start redressing the balance. Once we understand that, it will be much easier to develop more effective and efficient ways of helping learners.

It is only a start. It is an introductory collection. We hope intensely that the principle effect of this book will be to generate interest among other people and, hopefully, to encourage some of them to continue work in this area.

The Punctuation Project is hoping to act as a centre of information about the teaching and learning of punctuation. It can be contacted at:

The Didsbury School of Education,
Manchester Metropolitan University,
799 Wilmslow Road,
Didsbury,
Manchester M20 2RR, UK.

Phone: In UK (0161) 247 2069. Outside UK 44 161 247 2069
Fax: In UK (0161) 247 6392. Outside UK 44 161 247 6392
EMail: N.Hall@mmu.ac.uk
World Wide Web Page: http://b11.edu.aca.mmu.ac.uk/punctuation.html

1 Learning About Punctuation: An Introduction and Overview

NIGEL HALL

Introduction

This could be a very short chapter! To put it simply and straightfor-wardly, prior to this book it is possible to identify only a few studies which look in some way at how people (and with two exceptions, all are about children) learn to punctuate. It is rather like finding a desert in the middle of jungle. Most people could easily be overwhelmed by the huge quantities of books, articles, reports and teaching materials relating to becoming literate. Surely every conceivable aspect of becoming literate has been examined in great detail? Most have! You could spend a lifetime trying to read everything written about learning to spell, learning to handwrite, learning to compose, learning to read, learning about literature and so on. But, learning to punctuate...?

Perhaps a comparison with the literature on spelling will be helpful. I will even restrict myself to things written about learning to spell since 1970 when Charles Read published his seminal paper 'Pre-school children's knowledge of English phonology'. The number of books about learning to spell has reached substantial numbers and, just as importantly, so have the number of books about teaching spelling which draw on the research dealing with children's knowledge about spelling. The number of articles have to be counted in the thousands. If one added handbooks, instructional materials, reports, and more general pieces about spelling, then it would not be difficult to fill a reasonable-sized library with the literature and research about spelling development. What makes the comparison so important is that the direction of most of this writing is towards demonstrating that spelling knowledge is not simply learnt by rote, but is a generative response to the data surrounding a child. In other words children struggle to make sense of spelling by using their brains to create hypotheses about how the system works. Such an approach is, of course, consistent with a range of studies into many other aspects of literacy and psychological development. Thus, the issue of how children make sense of the phenomena of literacy becomes central to understanding how children learn to spell and can be taught to spell. No longer can the teaching of spelling be viewed as just a procedure involving direct instruction.

From where I sit as I write this piece I can see on my shelves about fifty books wholly and exclusively about spelling. Almost all these books are accounts of how children learn about spelling and how, in relation to those accounts, they can best be taught. I can see almost the same number of books about punctuation. It has taken me a long while to acquire fifty books wholly and exclusively about punctuation. Not one of them is about how people learn to punctuate. Apart from one of which examines the history of punctuation and one exploring the linguistics of punctuation, most are handbooks for competent adults and are, in essence, little more than descriptive accounts of the punctuation system and the rules for using it. They are the equivalent of the many handbooks for adults about spelling rules. They have to be for competent adults as almost all of them would be quite impenetrable to a basic learner. I can see about another forty books in my collection which are instructional books for children, essentially sets of exercises and this includes 'Punctuation Personified' first published in 1824. Not one of these is, as far as I can see, based on any research perspective about children's understanding of punctuation. Indeed, a study by Gentry (1981) found no agreement between US elementary school textbooks about how punctuation should be taught or the order in which it should be taught. In my filing cabinet I have about two hundred articles about punctuation. The topics they cover include the history of punctuation, the linguistics of punctuation, the nature of punctuation, punctuation in different languages, laments on the lack of punctuation, reports on standards of punctuation, tests on punctuation, the teaching of punctuation, and finally a very small number are about the learning of punctuation. No doubt I could add to this collection but I would soon be scraping the barrel and picking things just because of a fairly incidental mention of the word punctuation. In comparison to the rich and extensive literature about how children learn to spell and how, as a consequence, it should be taught, there is hardly anything about how children learn to punctuate.

One of the most significant illustrations of how limited are studies in beginning punctuation can be found in the review of punctuation by Little

(1984). This is an extremely thorough and extensive review, containing references to over 230 books and articles. These pieces cover a wide range of topics within the study of punctuation and quite a few are about, or related to, education. Although a number of these are ostensibly about children learning to punctuate, they are in fact about how children fail to punctuate, or about how they should be taught. Only two articles could be construed as being about the nature of the learning process, and Little does not review them as such. The topic of making sense of punctuation, of coming to make sense of the system, does not merit a mention in Little's review. This is not a criticism of Little; indeed any student of punctuation is in her debt. It does, however, indicate rather dramatically how recent are studies which focus upon the nature of the learning that takes place when people learn to punctuate.

Why has Punctuation been Neglected?

Why is the educational world drowning under research and writing about spelling, but apparently not even noticing the absence of studies about learning to punctuate? Of course, many authors and researchers have touched on punctuation in some way, and many books on writing or grammar include pages about punctuation, but so do they about spelling. However, what is clear is that almost none of the claims made in them about learning to punctuate are predicated upon a substantial research base about the learning of punctuation; it does not exist!

Yet, one thing is clear to all teachers of young children — young learners treat punctuation in the same generative way that they deal with spelling. The errors they make are clear evidence of serious attempts to make sense of how punctuation works. So why has spelling captured the research imagination and not punctuation? There are a number of possible answers to this question and to some extent these answers overlap.

One possible answer is that it might simply be an historical accident. If Charles Read had written in 1970 about punctuation instead of spelling, then would things have been different? Would the educational world have become enthused about punctuation in the same way as it has done about spelling? Or, was Read's choice of topic itself a consequence of the historical status of learning to spell? Learning to read and write in the West means learning to cope with an alphabetic system. What underpins the alphabetic system but a relationship between the sounds of speech and the letters of the alphabet. Thus, spelling is to a large extent a more salient feature of print than punctuation, as well as having been around for much longer than punctuation.

However, there is no doubt that the literacy education world was energised by Read's paper. For the first time someone was writing about literacy in ways which made sense of what teachers had always seen but never understood. It was also great fun for teachers to allow children to use their own spellings and observe the creativeness, effort, and intellectual struggle of children as they attempted to make sense of the spelling system. The negative side of this was that learning to write became for a while mostly about generating knowledge of the spelling system and other areas of writing development had less attention paid to them.

Spelling, anyway, seems to have more social significance than punctuation. While many commentators lump together their criticism of people's abilities to write 'correct English' and talk about problems with spelling, handwriting and punctuation, it is clear that poor spelling and handwriting arouse most ire. This may be because both are more visible than punctuation. Poor handwriting can be seen from several feet away; no-one has to read a text to see whether it is written legibly. Almost as easily, people who can spell are able spot a misspelling; it virtually jumps off the page. However, looking at the punctuation requires much more time and effort; the piece needs to be read carefully and such reading takes time.

Another possible reason is that spelling appears to most people to be quite straightforward. Spelling is essentially a closed system. At the end of the day, a spelling is almost always either right or wrong (but not always): one does not usually have a choice. Punctuation, on the other hand, is a relatively flexible system. It may use a relatively small number of marks but these can be used as dynamically as can any combination of words. In other words, there is choice involved and authors can consciously make these choices; many a paper has been written on the punctuation style of major literary figures (see Deneau, 1986). There has been an historical shift from authors tending to leave printers to put in the punctuation, to authors becoming very precise about how they want their work punctuated. According to Bullions (1846) the work of many authors was left 'to be pointed by the printers, who, from their constant practice, are supposed to have acquired a uniform mode of punctuation' (p. 152). Honan (1960) says 'One almost nods sympathetically at Byron's refusal to do his own final punctuating' (p. 97) and, according to Parkes (1992) Jean Jacques Rousseau, William Wordsworth and Charlotte Brontë all asked their respective publishers to correct the punctuation in their manuscripts. It is doubtful whether any modern author would leave responsibility for the punctuation of their text to a publisher or printer. The use of punctuation is now seen as part of the author's control over the sense of the text.

This assertion of control is perhaps recognition that, unlike spelling, punctuation is a relatively elusive notion, about which there is still much disagreement. Is punctuation based upon grammar, intonation, or a somewhat accidental history? Or, is it a combination of the three? There seems a general acceptance among authorities that to start with, punctuation was a means of marking the way a text should be read aloud. Indeed, according to Parkes (1992) in Roman manuscripts it was the reader who marked in the punctuation, not the writer. Somewhat paradoxically, it was partly because standards of education decreased that writers needed to put punctuation into texts; readers were less able to do it themselves. For many centuries punctuation was mainly elocutionary in orientation and it was not until the seventeenth century that serious debate about the function of punctuation began. During the eighteenth and nineteenth century there was a marked shift from elocutionary principles to syntactic principles and by 1840 an influential writer on punctuation was able to write:

> Many persons seem to consider points as being only the representatives of rhetorical pauses, — as showing merely those places in the utterance of a composition, in which time for breathing is required. But, though it is not denied that the points are, to a very great extent, serviceable to a reader in knowing when he should pause, occasion will frequently be taken, in the course of this work, to prove that the art of punctuation is founded more on a grammatical than on a rhetorical basis. (Wilson, 1844: vii–viii)

Nunberg (1990) provides a substantial linguistic explanation of why and how punctuation is grammatical and pertaining to written language rather than oral language.

However, despite a general consensus among writers on punctuation, the issue seems far from resolved. In 1972, Backscheider offered some rules for learners, of which the first was 'Most pauses can be heard — listen for the pauses.' (p. 875). Church (1967) says, 'These phonological rules of punctuation are either the basis of many of the conventional rules of punctuation, or they are at least compatible with them.' (p. 426). Furness (1960) maintains that 'the comma and semicolon are substitutes for pauses.' (p. 185) and Pflaum (1986) claims that 'Punctuation in writing is parallel to the intonation and suprasegmentals of oral language.' (p. 196) and Sopher (1977) asserts 'I propose to put forward the view that speech rhythm, adapted to the needs of written language, should in fact constitute the basis of sound punctuation' (p. 304). Perhaps all the positions are partly right and at the same time, partly wrong. As Partridge (1977) pointed out:

> Punctuation is predominantly constructional or grammatical or logi-

cal, yet it has what is in some ways a non-logical, non-grammatical element, necessitated by the part played in speech by intonation and pause, and in writing (or printing) by emphasis. (p. 7)

When authorities can disagree so strongly about what punctuation is and what it does, then it is not surprising that teachers should feel less secure about teaching it than they do about teaching spelling.

Punctuation, like all aspects of language, is a system in change. When spellings were enshrined in dictionaries they became relatively stable, particularly when the great national dictionaries — Oxford, Webster, Larousse — began to be developed during the nineteenth century (although I suspect I am not alone in thinking that spelling appears to have changed more during the last twenty years than had been the case during the previous one hundred years — Kwik Save has a lot to answer for!). Punctuation on the other hand is much more sensitive to stylistic change — indeed, it is often an agent of stylistic change. However, alongside change runs a kind of determinism that seeks to conserve rules, particularly where the teaching of punctuation is concerned. This creates some strange tensions as authors are led into awkward positions when offering models of 'good punctuation practice'.

Thorndike (1948: 537) wrote that 'learning to punctuate by imitation is beset with serious difficulties. The book most revered by children, the Bible, is punctuated badly'. The Bible he would have been referring to was, of course, the King James version first published in 1611, about the same time as Shakespeare's folios, the punctuation of which has also been ridiculed by many writers. As soon as anyone asserts good practice by offering examples from the great authors, it is possible to find from the pages of the most esteemed authors practices which confound convention and rule. McDermott (1990), writing a modern guide to punctuating practice attempted to get round this by stating 'The intention is to survey the current best practice in the use of punctuation by educated writers of English.' However, the logic of the position means that modern writers who agree with McDermott are 'educated' writers while those who disagree, even though they may be highly educated by anyone else's definition, are not.

This tension about what 'correct' punctuation is has never stopped publishers producing books, wholly and exclusively about punctuation, which offer accounts of the rules. Since 1800 there have been at least 150 such books produced (and this is almost certainly an underestimate and, anyway, does not include schools books). Many thousands of general grammar books will also have included sections with explicit accounts of punctuation rules. Is it perhaps the case that the abundance of such books, and the presence of punctuation teaching in almost all school books about grammar, led to people thinking that there were no problems with teaching punctuation? What is all the fuss about? All one had to do was apply the book to the child and the child would learn. As we will see in the next section — life is not so simple.

The Nature of the Problem for Children

Claims about standards

Children, or beginners of any age, starting to write and read face a formidable task. Just how formidable ought to be evident to anyone who is prepared to look. However, many people seem reluctant to do so. There is a peculiar kind of sanctimony behind the position that 'If I can do it, then anyone can do it'. Those who have learnt to do complex things in an apparently effortless way often fail to appreciate why others have difficulty. Learning to write means coming to grips with a system which is complex, operates on many levels, involves a range of physical and intellectual skills, is still evolving and, to put it mildly, is riddled with inconsistencies. Punctuation shares all these characteristics.

To judge from the reaction of current-day politicians, people in commerce and industry, as well as many parents, the failures to write English correctly are failures of contemporary education. Even if we leave aside the issue of evidence, what is clear is that complaints about standards of written English, and about punctuation in particular, are nothing new.

In 1900, Dickson, in discussing the rules of punctuation, said 'few understand, though many claim to but do not' (p. 2), and Lovell (1907) claimed, 'The putting-in of stops is the sort of business that everybody is supposed to do pretty well, but nobody is quite sure of.' Rourke (1915: 246) in writing about teaching punctuation, says:

> Bulk of thought and energy has been devoted to the problem, yet a tacit challenge is continually being offered to the methods of textbooks by the vagueness of which even the intelligent amateur exhibits when he tries to define the offices of the seven or eight marks which usage has maintained, and by the corresponding uncertainty of his practise.

In 1929 Symonds and Lee stated:

> Pupils are taught certain basic rules of punctuation and capitalisation as early as in the fourth grade; these same rules are repeated and practice on them continues through high school. Yet despite all this instruction, college teachers of English find conditions such as to evoke

their frequent complaints that students come to them unable to write with even mechanical correctness. (p. 461)

Coffin (1951) talks about many college students having never mastered punctuation, while Furness in 1960 claimed that 'investigations at the elementary school level show that mistakes in punctuation constitute from approximately one-third to more than one half of the total errors tabulated' (p. 185). McCorkle (1962) says 'but at the end of the semester we realize that the pupil is not appreciably nearer to an understanding of how to punctuate' and 'especially is this the case with regard to that elusive quality called "sentence sense," which results in a correct choice of comma or period for the end of a group of words making a complete, independent statement' (p. 673). Clearly, all the grammar books and straightforward applications of rule-based teaching were not being effective.

Equally clearly, failures to learn to punctuate at all levels are not a symptom of modern education but seem to have been a consistent feature across this century and before. This ought to be an indication that punctuation is more complicated than many people are prepared to acknowledge, and that simple solutions to the problem do not exist. It is, of course, the case that some children learn to punctuate relatively easily and experience few difficulties. However, this is no different to many other aspects of English, particularly spelling.

Educationalists have seldom agreed about when children should start to learn about punctuation or how they should begin. Milligan (1941) said 'probably no-one would seriously advocate the formal teaching of punctuation skills to children in the primary grades. On the other hand, no-one would deny primary children the opportunity to learn all they can about punctuation in situations which are part of their normal experiences'. In 1945 Salisbury clearly believed that a six-year-old should be able to cope with the major stops. She described a mythical child, Sally Peters, who in first grade should be able make a plan on paper or an outline in the mind and then 'expresses her ideas by putting down one sentence after another. When she is through with one sentence, she stops it with a period, and then she moves her hand along and starts another with a capital letter. It is just as simple as that.' Hill, writing in 1984, tells of a recent time in Australia 'when the Course of Study for Schools prescribed that every child at the end of Grade 2 should be able to write a sentence beginning with a capital letter and ending with a full stop'. Now, in the UK, we find a National Curriculum demanding that an average seven-year-old is able to demarcate accurately a piece of prose using full stops and capital letters. All the above positions are not, as will by now be clear, based upon any research evidence about how children learn to punctuate.

Claims about teaching

How should punctuation knowledge be achieved? The disagreements are just as strong. There are those who see punctuation knowledge being achieved through learning rules, there are those who see it as learned through being allowed to write, and there are those who see it as happening through imitating the examples of reading. As more children were taught to write so there was more attention paid to the rules which would govern the use of punctuation in the act of writing. These rules were almost always grammatical and their numbers reached large quantities. Salisbury (1939) reported that when she left school in 1910 to go to an academy near Boston, she spent a year learning 157 rules for punctuation. This typical dependence upon punctuation rules was criticised by Moe (1913) who said:

> Sweeping, for example, is a simple operation, and yet one could imagine the result of writing out explicit rules for holding the broom and passing it over the carpet and giving them to the little girl to learn by heart, instead of putting a real broom in her hands and showing her the motions of sweeping. (p. 104)

Explanations about punctuation

Perhaps the problems facing the beginner, and particularly the youngest children, can be best illuminated by considering the data about punctuation which is presented to them. The English section of the National Curriculum demands that, by the age of seven, young children are able to demarcate sentences using full stops and capital letters. How does one explain to a young child where to put a full stop? The simple answer is 'you put a full stop at the end of a sentence'.

At first sight this seems unproblematic. However, it is a rather awkward definition because it presupposes that young children know what a sentence is. Not only is the evidence clear that most young children have a very confused notion of what a sentence is, but many of them, particularly when they start writing, have no notion at all of the concept 'sentence'. This is illustrated rather clearly by the National Curriculum not requiring grammatical knowledge of the sentence until well after children are asked to demarcate sentences using full stops and capital letters. To sum up, the children are required to learn something that cannot adequately be explained to them because they would not understand the explanations.

The fully grammatical sentence is a unit of written language, not spoken language (Kress, 1982; Nunberg, 1990). It is relatively uncommon for speech to be demarcated into fully grammatical sentences. When it does happen it is usually because the speaker has prepared a speech, probably by writing it down. It is noticeable that politicians who in public speeches tend to use grammatical sentences, often fail to do so when interviewed. Some politicians are notorious for their failure to construct complete grammatical sentences in speech. These failures are not because politicians are stupid, uneducated or unable to construct grammatical sentences. It is simply because conversational speech does not work like written language. Speech, and particularly conversation, often contains hesitations, truncated sentences, use of gesture to replace words, incomplete meanings, half-sentences run together and changes of tack in mid-sentence. There are no full stops in speech! On the whole, the other speaker does not experience the conversation as a mess; it is part of the way in which conversation works. We grow up learning to cope with speech as it exists.

Children, during the first years of their life, grow up in a world which is highly oral. Their only access to written language might be through having books read to them. For the most part they grow up using conversation as they hear it. They have no knowledge at all that when speech is written down it has the potential to be divided into special units called sentences. Thus, when young children approach writing for the first time they do not start with a preconceived notion of sentence.

So, how do teachers help children learn to place full stops at the ends of sentences when the children do not yet understand the notion of sentence? Teachers' strategies tend to fall into four categories although, of course, many teachers use a combination of these in their classroom work. These categories are grammaticality, meaningfulness, pausing and facilitating intuition.

For the most part, traditional grammarians accept that defining the 'sentence' is a relatively straightforward process. Linguists see this as a much more problematic event, and defining 'sentence' is an issue that recurs frequently in the literature of linguistics. Nevertheless, in an everyday sense, books on grammar and punctuation have a strong measure of agreement about grammatical definitions. However, this agreement is certainly at the expense of simplicity where a five- or six-year-old child is concerned. Carey (1958, but originally published in 1939) says:

> Every school boy knows that full-stops come at the end of sentences; and seeing that a sentence has got to contain at least one main clause, with its own finite verb, quite apart from any subordinate clause that

may be added, one would have thought that this was about all that
need be said on the subject. (p. 23)

This explanation is one of the less problematic ones, but nevertheless one
wonders which schoolboys he was writing about. Even in 1939 it would
certainly not have been state-educated five-year-olds at the start of their
writing careers. It is doubtful that five-year-olds would make anything of
'main clause', 'finite verb', subordinate clause', let alone the individual
words 'clause', 'verb', 'subordinate' or 'finite'. It would be interesting to
know what most people understand by these technical terms, if they
understand anything at all about them. As indicated above, there is
something of a problem about grammatical explanations; they are often
more complex than the phenomenon they are attempting to define.
Certainly few beginning writers start with an explicit grammatical knowledge of their own language. Successful usage does not indicate the ability
to intellectually deconstruct language.

Another common strategy of teachers is to say something like 'a sentence
is a complete thought'. In fact a recent adult handbook book titled 'Grammar
and Punctuation' (which had better remain anonymous) offers on page
seven a definition of a sentence. 'A sentence is a group of words which
makes complete sense'. On page one of that book is a group of words
between a capital letter and a full stop. The words are: 'Thus less
punctuation is used'. Does that sentence on its own make 'complete' sense
to anyone? The notion of 'complete sense' is highly ambiguous. Sentences
can, of course contain only one word: 'No!' In context it might make
complete sense but as a sentence on its own its meaning is quite obscure.
The problem being highlighted is one of what can count as complete sense,
and this has to be seen in the context of trying to explain to children what
complete sense can possibly mean. Does a word have complete sense? Does
a sentence have compete sense if it is part of a paragraph, or a chapter or a
book? At what point can a reader or writer claim that something possesses
complete sense? The total ambiguity of the words means that it is rather
unhelpful as an explanation for children. Indeed one writer (Kress, 1982,
and see later this chapter) has shown that children group words into
meaningful chunks when those words often add up to much more than a
single sentence.

An alternative explanation, and one of the commonest, offered to young
children about the placing of full stops refers to a relationship between
length of pause between sentences and the notion of 'punctuation'.
Children are told 'You put a full stop where there is a long pause', or 'You

put a full stop when you take a long breath'. However there are two major problems with this type of explanation.

The first is the presumed relationship between 'pausing' and punctuation. It is a very inconsistent relationship. Oral speech does not always have pauses between those items which would in written language be seen as the boundaries between sentences, while it often does have pauses where no punctuation would be placed in written language. This is so much so that these days even when people are reading aloud they often do not leave pauses between sentences. It has become increasingly difficult to follow some news reports because of this. Not only are sentences run together without pauses, but so are major topic items. Politicians are extremely skilled at not using conventional intonation and avoiding using pauses in order to prevent interviewers from interrupting them. Thus, if children were to truly follow the rule and put punctuation when they heard pauses, they would often find themselves in trouble.

The second problem is that it relates more directly to reading rather than writing. For it to relate to writing, the writer has to be very conscious of a reader who needs to make perfect sense of what is written. If one looks at *Punctuation Personified* (1824), the first punctuation book specifically for children, then it is clear that pausing at punctuation was to teach children to use punctuation when reading aloud. It begins:

> Young Robert could read, but he gabbled so fast;
> And ran on with such speed, that all meaning he lost.
> Till one Morning he met Mr. Stops by the way,
> Who advis'd him to listen to what he should say.

Later in the book the child is introduced to the system of counting the length of pause for each stop.

> In him the PERIOD we behold,
> Who stands his ground whilst four are told.

while for a comma

> Yet so BRIEF is each pause, that he merely counts ONE.

Of course, at that time far more children were taught to read than were ever taught to write, and reading was primarily something that was oral rather than silent. It is, however, still possible to come across adults who were taught the 'rule of four' not so many years ago when they were at school, but it is only a rule of oral reading and even then, leads to a very strained type of reading. Most people do not read aloud and it must be accepted that reading aloud is not an identical process to reading silently; as Carey (1958) stated:

It must be remembered that the needs of the eye are not exactly the same as those of the voice. (p. 15)

Reading aloud is a relatively unnatural activity — we normally read silently and usually fairly swiftly. Thus, the way we most frequently experience written language bears a strained relationship with the oral rendition of that same language, and the ways in which we normally use speech differ even more from formal written language. Punctuation/pause relationships can sometimes work, but they can also be very wrong. McDermott (1990) sums it up when he writes:

An unhelpful legacy of this attitude is the nonsense that different stops represent different lengths of pause. (p. 22)

It is even questionable whether reading needs punctuation. As Smith (1982: 154) commented:

The importance of punctuation is greatly overrated. Early Greeks managed to write and read the first Western alphabetic language without periods, spaces between words, or capital letters (or rather without lower-case letters) ...other punctuation marks with which we are familiar did not appear for centuries.

It is interesting to note that research into children's use of punctuation when reading is almost non-existent (for an exception see Perera in this volume).

Beginning writers do three things which make the explanation of rests or pauses somewhat problematic. First, as beginning writers they are likely to be pausing between every word as they make their marks on paper, so should they put a full stop between every word (and, of course, some do — see Chapter 2)? Secondly, they tend to write only short pieces, often only one line long, and so there is little, if any, need to pause when reading them. Thirdly, even when they write longer pieces with no punctuation they seem to have no trouble whatsoever putting in appropriate pauses when they read their piece aloud; they know how it should be read! In our work on The Punctuation Project we have found so many children who can tell you that a full stop means you take a rest but who put no full stops into even quite lengthy pieces of writing. When one six-year-old child was asked why there were no full stops in his two-page piece, he replied, 'Well, I opened my mouth really wide and took a huge amount of air into my mouth so I was able to read it without stopping.'

Pausing is, of course, part of intonation, and we have already seen in a previous section that there is considerable dispute between authorities on the extent to which punctuation represents intonational or grammatical relationships. This dispute was ignored by the authors of a leaked draft document relating to the teaching of punctuation at Key Stage 1 (5–7 years) of the British National Curriculum. It stated: 'Pupils should be taught that punctuation replaces the intonation and emphasis available to a speaker and is, therefore, essential to effective writing'.

Some teachers accept the extraordinary difficulty of the above types of explanations and try to get children to intuit a notion of 'sentence'. This is done partly by giving the children good experience of reading text with punctuation, partly through correction, partly through offering demonstrations (perhaps through writing on the board), and partly through exercises asking children to place full stops in written text. The expectation is that children will develop a *feel* for what counts as a 'sentence'. To some extent children inevitably have to do this, as it is difficult to see how the explanations offered by teachers can be unambiguous.

This strategy, despite a degree of success, clearly does not work for everyone and one has to have a degree of sympathy for the man, described by Parsons (1915: 598) 'who filled a page or two of his *magnum opus* with all sorts of punctuation marks and appended a note asking his readers to choose from the collection of commas, semi-colons, exclamation points, and question marks just what was necessary to interpret the various sentences of the book'.

What has been written in this section indicates that there are many opinions about learning to punctuate. What is missing is evidence!

Studies of Learning about Punctuation

Given that there are so few studies of how people learn to punctuate, it is worthwhile spending time examining these in some detail and considering the extent to which they add up to a coherent body of knowledge. Such an examination should also clarify areas where future study could be profitably directed.

While studies about learning to punctuate are mostly fairly recent, it seems that the first people to note that learning to punctuate involved children formulating incorrect, but nevertheless reasonable hypotheses were Pressey & Campbell (1933). After studying errors in capitalisation by ninth-grade children, they wrote that 'the first, rather unexpected point, is that the errors in capitalisation were in large part explainable, logical and understandable; they were far from being random or senseless' (p. 1970). They gave examples of this 'explainable, logical and understandable' thinking by the children. For instance:

If God is capitalized, why not the things God does?

If the writer is thinking of a particular street, island, river or town, why shouldn't he capitalize it even though its actual name does not appear?

If the names of certain people, such as Puritans, Jews, Republicans, are capitalised, why not the names of other groups such as pirates, lawyers, companions?

These children were ninth-grade children, that is aged about 14, and were still trying to make sense of rules that for them were often internally inconsistent, or seemed to contradict other logical positions. However 1933 was clearly not the time for this interesting finding to be examined in a more creative way and the world had to wait a long time before this generative principle was rediscovered.

For Pressey and Campbell the finding was something of an accidental discovery. Ferreiro & Teberosky (1984) approached their studies with a better sense of anticipation and a solid theoretical foundation. They are psychologists who come from a Piagetian tradition. Thus, their theoretical position assumed certain ways of thinking by young children, and indeed, compared with the 14-year-olds studied by Pressey and Campbell, their children were very young; Ferreiro & Teberosky carried out their investigations using a range of children in Argentinian pre-schools.

Ferreiro & Teberosky studied some aspects of punctuation development as part of a much wider, systematic study of young children's literacy development. Prior to their investigations many people working in literacy education had assumed that children before schooling knew nothing about literacy and that consequently the task of schooling was to 'teach' children about literacy. Ferreiro & Teberosky started from the position that children were critically interested in their world, and that things of great significance to the adults around them were not ignored. They wrote:

> We have searched unsuccessfully in this literature for reference to children themselves, thinking children who seek knowledge, children we have discovered through Piagetian theory. The children we know are learners who actively try to understand the world around them, to answer questions the world poses...it is absurd to imagine that four- or five-year-old children growing up in an urban environment that displays print everywhere (on toys, on billboards and road signs, on their clothes, on TV) do not develop any ideas about this cultural object until they find themselves sitting in front of a teacher. (p. 12)

The general claim made by Ferreiro & Teberosky, once they had completed their studies, was that in learning about the social object that we call literacy, children progress through a series of stages, as a result of which knowledge about literacy is progressively differentiated, and comes to approximate more and more to conventional literacy knowledge. The propulsive mechanism to move through the stages is a biological one; a drive to make sense of phenomena in the world, and by exercising this drive upon literacy children build notions of what literacy is and how it works. A critical part of this theory is that the stages through which children pass are hierarchically organised. Thus early stages are broad and relatively undifferentiated, but are nevertheless fundamental. For example, children have to discriminate between the marks we call drawing and the marks we call writing before any further differentiation of the 'writing marks' can take place.

When Ferreiro & Teberosky started their study they had not anticipated that the children would be capable of discriminating between letters and punctuation marks, but as they became more aware of the knowledge that the children, in particular the middle-class children, had about literacy, they added this area to their study. It seems that each child was shown a printed page from a storybook and asked about the marks that were not letters (the authors do not give precise details about how the responses were initiated). The children's ages (in the examples given) were four and five, although six-years-olds were examined as well.

Ferreiro & Teberosky give what they call a 'strictly descriptive classification' of their results. However, at the same time they claim that description enables them to distinguish levels. These levels move from:

(1) No distinction between punctuation marks and letters or numbers.
(2) Some marks begin to be differentiated. Full stops, hyphens, colons and … are labelled as 'dots', and are seen as different from all the other writing marks.
(3) Punctuation marks which are letter-like continue to be viewed as letters/numbers, but all the others are different.
(4) Most punctuation marks are discriminated from letters or numbers. Some confusions continue between marks which are very like letters, for instance ';' can be confused with 'i'.
(5) There is a clear distinction between letters and punctuation, and the children begin to use labels, speaking of 'marks' and sometimes actual punctuation-mark labels.

A number of points must be made about the claims regarding this sequence. The first is that the sequence covers a relatively small amount of movement. Thus even at Stage 5 there is no suggestion that the children understand in any conventional sense what punctuation is and what it does. The children at the first four stages have no sense of any function existing for punctuation marks, and even at the fifth stage explanations are description rather than explanation. Secondly, unlike all other researchers, they have looked at children prior to formal schooling, although all their children were at pre-schools. Finally, as very few examples are offered by Ferreiro & Teberosky, and there is almost no description of the situation in which children were doing their learning, it is difficult to interpret what they do offer.

Ferreiro & Teberosky do explicitly claim that observation of the responses across age and social groups indicates a clear progression. Thus, the majority of the four-year-olds showed no discrimination, while the all of the five- and six-year-olds were capable of some discrimination. However, the claim for a 'progression' is not as clear cut as it might seem. In the section of their book where they discuss knowledge about punctuation, they say:

> The period, the question mark, and the exclamation point are the first to be introduced in initial school instruction.

This introduces a critical element — the effect of environment. Ferreiro & Teberosky do acknowledge that the environment is an element, talking about punctuation being non-deducible, socially transmitted knowledge. However, the one thing that never features in their account is any consideration of the nature of the interaction with the pre-school. It is possible to suggest that the reason the four-year-olds did not know about the use of punctuation marks was because people, parents and pre-school teachers, did not bring it to their attention. Perhaps the expectation was different for the five- and six-year-olds and people started to mention it or expect children to notice it. Thus, it is difficult to tell the extent to which the age differences are the result of some cognitive difference or the consequence of the differing social experience of the children (and this is specially important given that even the children at their Stage 5 were simply labelling rather than using or explaining punctuation). This is a significant question for Piagetian theorists as there has always been a debate between those who suggest that ages and stages cannot be hurried, and those who suggest that environment can make significant difference to the rate and manner of children's intellectual development (Donaldson, 1978).

It is worth noting that the studies carried out by Ferreiro & Teberosky involved removing children from their classrooms and subjecting them to questions and activities led by the research team members. These activities were somewhat decontextualised and deliberately 'conflictive or potentially conflictive' and would have been outside any prior experience of the children. The authors claim that their procedures involved 'interpreting the alphabetic code as it appears in the daily world', but one has to ask how often four- and five-year-old children are confronted in daily life by exercises of the sort devised for this study.

In a direct way the impact of their work upon studies in punctuation has been minimal. Later studies in young children's understanding of punctuation make little or no reference to their work. However the totality of their studies have had considerable impact upon the way researchers and teachers think more generally about the development of literacy and their book must be one of the most frequently cited. What they did achieve was a coherent account of the development of literacy knowledge, of which punctuation has, necessarily, to be a part.

Appearing almost simultaneously with the English translation of the Ferreiro & Teberosky study was one by Cordiero, Giacobbe & Cazden (1983), another version of which appeared as Cazden, Cordiero & Giacobbe (1985). These were both based upon data collected from the first grade classroom of Giacobbe. The study focused upon possessive apostrophes, quotation marks and full stops, and used data collected from the twenty-two children during the whole school year. Compared with the Ferreiro & Teberosky study, these children were slightly older, but perhaps more significantly were in a classroom where it was expected that children would learn about and use punctuation. As a consequence there is some data offering a perspective on classroom practice. Accompanying the children's writing were notes made by Giacobbe about when particular skills were taught (and sometimes retaught). Both the children's work and the teacher's written records were examined retrospectively. The authors offer typical comments made by Giacobbe to teach any punctuation points, although it seems likely that these are 'typical' rather than precise as they were not documented as such during the year but offered as retrospective examples. Thus, there has to be a question mark about what was actually said by Giacobbe to each child. The records indicated that during the year only six children were taught the use of the possessive apostrophe and six the use of quotation marks. Full stops were taught and retaught to 13 children. The typical pattern suggested was that Giacobbe read the child's story aloud without pauses and when the author objected said 'You read it the way you want it to sound. When you come to a stop, that's probably where you need to put a period' (1983). It might be worth considering the ambiguity of this statement in relation to the analysis of a teaching moment offered by Arthur in Chapter 7.

The authors found five frequent patterns of usage of full stops. They found interword, endline, endpage, phrase structure and correct usage (presumably meaning grammatical sentence differentiation). Importantly they state, 'All the children tried out more than one of these hypotheses, often more than one in a single story' (1985: 329). It is questionable whether the elements noted by the researchers were actually specific hypotheses or simply manifestations of deeper level hypotheses. In other words, the children may not have been using different hypotheses in one piece, but using one hypothesis which generated marks in different places, some of which, by accident, were conventionally correct. They claim that children intuitively seemed to know something about the structural status of parts of their writing, and that punctuation, while often incorrect in conventional terms, was sometimes placed at syntactically significant points.

Surprisingly, in view of the claim made that the study was a longitudinal one (in the 1983 paper it is called a 'longitudinal analysis'), nowhere in the article is there any description of how change took place over time. We are simply told that most children after some teaching were more accurate than before, but over what time period we do not know. Unlike Ferreiro & Teberosky who attempted to showed how children's beliefs changed over time, the authors of this study make no reference as to how the claimed hypotheses were used by children at different times. The authors say at one point:

> Teachers should realize that progress — while real — is not steady. Especially with periods, alternative hypotheses co-exist, and seemingly correct usage in one composition is followed by errors of both omission and commission in the next. (1985: 123)

However they fail to give any data about how this variation in usage occurred across the year. Knowing that children may have used more than one strategy in one piece, or that the use was not consistent, does not mean that more fundamental changes might not be occurring over a time period as long as a year.

The children wrote on average 272 sentences during the year but unfortunately we are not told the average number of sentences per piece, although we are told that is an average of 1.5 a day. It also appears (but only in Cordiero, 1988) that the first-grader's work included drafts as well as finished work, and it is unclear whether the use of punctuation in draft work might be different from that in finished work. As, to some extent, a real understanding of period placement is likely to be linked to writing the equivalent of more than one sentence, it would have been useful to have known how many pieces went beyond the single sentence. Neither do they give any other background information about what may have contributed to the children's learning. They, nevertheless, do acknowledge that 'children have many sources of information in addition to the teacher'.

Cordeiro (1988) compared the data collected in Giacobbe's classroom with data collected in a third-grade classroom, concentrating on period placement by the young writers. There were some clear differences between the two groups although there was little difference between the two groups in the extent to which they correctly used periods at the ends of sentences. (This similarity is not as surprising as it may seem at first sight. As suggested above, many of the first-grade pieces of writing may have been only one sentence and even using a rule like 'the period comes at the end' the first graders would score many correct placements. On the other hand, the third-graders may have used many more complex sentences with ensuing difficulties in sorting out sentence and intra-sentence boundaries.) The differences came in the errors made by the children. Third graders made mostly errors that Cordiero calls 'phrasal misplacements'; they used periods in the wrong places but almost always at phrase boundaries. First-graders on the other hand made many more errors related to lineness, wordness and pageness rather than syntactic categories (something that was not made clear in the 1983 or 1985 reports).

While Cordiero's analysis points out some gross differences which reveal a clear move to textual punctuation, it still, despite having access to two sets of data collected across a one-year period, omits to look any closer at how these changes were taking place during the year and how different children were moving towards making sense of punctuation.

Edelsky (1983) undertook a descriptive study of the writing development of nine first-grade, nine second-grade, and eight third-grade children enrolled in a bilingual programme. All the children's in-class writing for one week was collected four times during one school year. (A total of 525 pieces were collected from the children, which works out at an average of almost five pieces per child for each week of data collection, an average of just over 19 pieces for the four weeks of data collection — although the number of pieces collected from each child ranged from 10 to 31.) In addition, data deriving from teachers' and aides' responses in interviews, day-long classroom observations, test scores and school records, and more general school and district data was used. A range of phenomena was analysed and one of these was what Edelsky termed non-spelling conventions — punctuation and segmentation. The children were in what is termed a 'whole-language' classroom, although some of the practices described might now seem rather formal for a current perspective on what constitutes a whole-language classroom. Nevertheless, Edelsky says there was no direct teaching of segmentation going on in the classrooms studied although there was some for punctuation. Edelsky restricted herself to commenting upon three aspects of punctuation. In the following notes I concentrate on the punctuation rather than the segmentation.

Edelsky chose to concentrate her analysis on three types of unconventional punctuation: a period at the end of every line; a hyphen separating syllables or words; and a capital letter at the start and period at the end of a piece but no internal punctuation. It is not clear why these were chosen, why other uses were ignored or why there was no examination of how the children appropriately used punctuation. Several types of unconventional punctuation were actually found: end of line; hyphens separating syllables or words; no internal punctuation; capital letters at the beginning of each line; invented designs to separate lines or to end pieces; a full stop after certain words or phrases; numbers on every line; a full stop at the end of each page.

Differences did emerge between the three grades, although differences occurring within grades are much more difficult to interpret. The general trend was that there was a shift towards more conventional punctuation, or what she called 'textual punctuation' as the grade increased and away from punctuation focused upon 'local features' (such as line relatedness). In this respect Edelsky & Cordiero (1988) found similar movements across grades. However, such a statement begs more questions than it answers.

Interpreting these first two general points is very difficult, and both the methodology used for collecting data and the style of analysis compound the difficulty. The paper gives no evidence about the behaviours of any single child; the tables combine data from the different groups. Thus, the patterns of any individual changes are obscured. Such combining may be necessary as four one-week collections do not add up to a lot of data from each individual child. As many of the first-grade pieces will be very short, then there is, for some children, very little data to analyse. Without consistent data from individual children, and data drawn from over more extended periods than one week, it is difficult to interpret the nature of any changes that might appear to take place. Indeed it would not be difficult for the data from a very small number of children to distort the overall picture (as indeed happened where segmentation was concerned and 130 out of 148 responses of one type were produced by only five children).

The one instance where Edelsky does give information about particular children turns out to be very interesting and raises an important issue. In the second grade class, two children arrived from Mexico and although they were older than their class peers they had received very little formal schooling. These children, at the start, wrote no more than their names or strings of letters. Edelsky suggests that it is experience with literacy not age which influences change and she speculates about whether much older beginning writers would forgo hypothesising about punctuation. In one sense though this is a somewhat redundant issue as stated by Edelsky. No-one seems to be suggesting that children, or adults, who have no or virtually no experience of literacy are going to start by being concerned with punctuation.

The significant issue is much more to do with the relationship between actual experiences with literacy and how understanding of punctuation develops, and Edelsky is able to make some very interesting suggestions about this relationship. First-grade children wrote journals and letters. 'Children were on their own to a greater extent during journal writing. The letters, on the other hand, would be sent.' She claims that this may have resulted in more unconventional segmentation in the journals. On the other hand, in the second-grade class, letters were usually reports on social studies work and may have been more difficult for the children than other kinds of writing, thus causing less attention to be paid to segmentation and punctuation. She also speculates that differences in materials may have influenced punctuation. In her study the use of Spanish or English was an important variable. Because the children wrote initially mostly in Spanish fewer non-textual errors occurred in the English data. It is also the case that as the children were Spanish-speaking most of their information about writing in English will have come from printed English texts where use of punctuation would have been fairly visible. Although Edelsky does not offer too much information about these effects (one week collections of data are inevitably limited), her work powerfully suggests just how valuable consistent collection of such data might be.

A rather different strand emerges from the work of Shaughnessy (1977). Shaughnessy studied basic writers (older students who for various reasons had problems with writing). These students were either at college and experiencing difficulties or enrolled in basic education classes. Adult basic writers have some different problems to beginning writers. Adult basic writers have the double burden of having to both learn and unlearn. However, what is particularly significant is that these writers are, for the most part, learners whose failures are attributable to early schooling. Adult basic writers have a partial knowledge of punctuation.

> The problem lies, however, in their partialness, in the writers' unawareness of a punctuation 'system,' in their fragments of misinformation that have by now become trusted stratagems in the battle with the page. (p. 18)

However, she also identifies an aspect which may be fully shared by young children.

> The small marks of punctuation, after all, don't look very important. They don't seem to say much either, at least nothing that the writer doesn't already know through his 'writer's ear,' which guides him in both the writing and reading of his own sentences. (p. 27)

Children are notorious for being able to read text without attending to punctuation. Arthur, in an aspect of her work not reported in her chapter in this book, presented children with two texts which were identical except that in one the punctuation had been omitted or changed (upper-case letters became lower-case letters). The children when asked to indicate any difference completely failed to notice the punctuation changes. They noticed minute marks on the edge of the paper, and talked about some letters being slightly fainter than others, but none of these six-year-olds mentioned the punctuation until they had it pointed out to them. She also observed a five-year-old who wrote a whole page with no punctuation. When asked to read it back the child did so perfectly. When asked about the full stops, the child said 'I don't need any', which was, of course, true.

The emphasis in Shaughnessy's work was in examining the nature of the errors made by basic writers with a view to developing more appropriate teaching strategies. Although to some extent people had been doing this throughout the century, the main contribution of Shaughnessy was to use the errors not to complain about failure of students but to understand and interpret the behaviours they represented. She understood that unconventional punctuation was not straightforwardly wrong, but was highly informative and gave particular insight into the punctuation strategies used by the learners. She adopted a mainly textual analysis to do this; a methodology which can be powerful but also contains some limitations. For instance, there is no evidence in her section on punctuation that she explored the students declared reasons for their punctuating behaviours. That such an approach is highly informative is revealed by the work of Ivanic (1988, and see her chapter in this book).

Unlike the work of Ferreiro & Teberosky, the work of Shaughnessy has had a direct impact upon subsequent work, and virtually all the succeeding researchers' studies acknowledge the significance of her work for them and make the analysis of errors a significant part of their study.

On the whole, only Ferreiro & Teberosky of the above authors have taken a developmental stance towards their topic and it seems that Kress (1982 and rev 1992) is the only person to take a longer term, directional perspective. Kress, however, did not do so as part of an attempt to understand punctuation but did so while examining the development of the notion 'sentence'. Kress views the primary direction of development in children's writing as being a move towards mastery of the sentence, both as an object with a distinct internal structure and as an object which has relationships with other units of a larger text. Clearly what Kress is saying has major implications for children's understanding of sentence terminal punctuation.

Kress offers a range of examples which, he claims, show children operating at different stages of comprehension of the notion 'sentence'. His data are not truly developmental. He offers virtually no information about the children who produced his examples or the situations in which they were produced. The examples came from different children and, apart from one example, we do not know out of what teaching the texts emerged or what help may have been given. Thus, while Kress has a notion of what development looks like and has chosen examples which illustrate his claim, he has not shown us that any individual child has moved through his proposed sequence. Nevertheless, his ideas are powerful and offer a way of making sense of some aspects of punctuation that is not available from other research.

His suggestion is that learning about sentences is a task of developing textual knowledge rather than syntactic knowledge: 'to the extent that they have become aware of them, sentences in early writing are primarily textual units, and that the child's attempt to work towards a definition of the sentence is a textual rather than a syntactic process. It is a matter of handling discourse, text rather than isolated syntactic units.' (Kress, 1992: 75)

Kress suggests that as children become aware of the need to organise text and aware that punctuation has a role in doing so, they explore ways of separating out major units. However, their criteria for doing so are not syntactic ones but derive from topic integrity. In other words, each unit that is marked by punctuation has integrity as a topic. The topics may or may not correspond to syntactic sentences; they may be phrases which to a child represent a complete notion, or they may spread across what adults would see as several syntactic sentences because the child sees the elements as being part of one topic.

As an example Kress offers a short piece 'Our trip to Ayers rock'. In this extract from it the child wrote:

> On Friday 1st July we all got in the bus and waved to Miss Martyn. We're off I thought, there was lots of merry talk in the bus. Tracey was telling some people that the bus would pass her house 'there it is' said Tracey but it soon went by. (Kress, 1992: 81)

Clearly sentences two and three cover units that would be separated into distinct sentences by an experienced writer. Kress suggests that for this child the second sentence forms a topically sound unit which might be termed 'the beginning of the journey', while the third sentence might be called 'Tracey's house' and as such both are seen as units requiring differentiating punctuation. Kress makes the point that it is not lack of syntactic complexity which prevents young children from forming conventionally punctuated sentences, even the youngest children use a rich range of syntactic forms, but of what belongs and does not belong together in terms of meaning. Of course, many writers about punctuation and grammar do offer to younger readers (and in some cases all readers) a definition of a sentence that has as a major component 'a group of words that makes complete sense on its own' (Gee & McClelland, 1992: 2). Kress is clearly suggesting that children may have their own notions of what counts as 'complete sense' and that these may or may not be related to more conventional notions.

It has been suggested (Goodman, 1980) that in learning to become literate a child, to some extent, rediscovers what it took society centuries to work out. In this context it is worth noting that in the fourth century when punctuation was beginning to be introduced into texts by 'grammatici' or teachers of literacy, the definition of a 'sententiae' was, according to Parkes (1992), 'A thought or opinion'. Parkes suggests that the word which ultimately gave us 'sentence' originally meant the substance or meaning of a group of words rather than the words themselves, and that the Latin word 'period' means 'In prose, an utterance or complete rhetorical structure which expresses a single idea or sententia'. While Kress is reminding us that a child's notion of 'making sense' is not necessarily that of an adult or a grammarian, it may be the case that, to some extent, a child does first what writing societies did first.

The sequence for Kress is one that moves from a relatively undifferentiated text, through texts which have units governed by a child's notion of topic relatedness, towards texts which are organised into syntactic sentences. Such a sequence may take a long time and Kress's analysis allows us to look at the development of sentence punctuation as being a long-term process — something which extends well beyond early childhood.

There are a number of points that need to made about this analysis, many of which Kress makes himself. The first is that there are many influences at work upon children's understanding of sentence and sentence punctuation. Children will be hearing messages from teachers which may be about sense, about breathing or about grammar (or about all three — see Arthur's chapter in this book). Younger children may be hearing concentrated messages about full stops going 'at the end of sentences' long before they have any notion of sentence. Kress says 'it is quite possible that 'sentence' has no real meaning for the child, and that 'line' may have as great a significance or greater for the child as a sentence' (1982: 72). Certainly 'line' may be important for younger children who have limited experience of writing, whose first experience of writing was copying single lines, and whose experience of reading is often from books which have single lines of text on a page. Thus the shifts that Kress discusses could be well-hidden under children's texts which are influenced by these other constraints.

Secondly, children may not be consciously aware of how they are organising their texts. Thus when discussing their reasons for punctuating sentences children may offer a range of explanations (or none at all) which do not fully represent the underlying intellectual moves that they have made.

Thirdly, different forms of text may yield different kinds of punctuation strategies. In his chapter, Kress looks at some non-narrative writing undertaken by young children. There is a strong suggestion that non-narrative writing, particularly description or report, may lead to apparently better sentence punctuation as it is relatively easier for a child to segment a fact about something than it is to separate an element from a continuous narrative. Thus a child may find it easier to write:

> the mices enemy are cats and owls. the mices eat all kinds of think. Mices are little animals. people set traps to catch mouse. mouses liv in holes in the skirting board. (1982: 77)

than to tease out a distinct element of a narrative text. This, however, does seem to assume that the child is using simple rather than complex sentences to capture distinct attributes.

Fourthly, Kress's ideas have yet to be examined in any extended study of writing development. Although his work has been mentioned by some of the above authors, no-one yet seems to have set out to assess the developmental validity of Kress's ideas. Possibly, this is because most of the above authors were working with quite young children and, in order to see the movements that Kress implies, there is a need for children to be writing a quantity of text that is sufficient to merit division into a number of sentences. This seems unfortunate as it is, at the time of writing, thirteen years since Kress's book was first published and his ideas are powerful, linguistically interesting and certainly do offer an important additional facet to making sense of a child's knowledge of the punctuation system.

Wilde (1988) reported on a study of six native American children while they were in third and forth grade. The classroom was visited each week, observations were made of the children writing (some sessions were video-taped) and some interviews with children were carried out. In this classroom there was virtually no instruction in punctuation and the teaching process was relatively traditional rather than process oriented. All the stories written by the children were computer-analysed. The six children produced 215 stories, containing 13,793 words. There were 1405 uses of punctuation, 1254 of them conventionally correct and Wilde claimed to determine that there were 1001 omissions of punctuation. Despite the availability of data across a two-year period, Wilde, like the other studies in which data were collected longitudinally, does not report longitudinally in respect of anything except very gross differences between the third and fourth grade (although for some information about this see Wilde's chapter in this book). The decision to only collect stories is perhaps unfortunate given the suggestions of Kress that different kinds of writing might yield different usage of punctuation. Nevertheless, the data show some interesting points.

It was clear that these children found punctuation more difficult than spelling and that some marks were easier to use than others (full stops were correctly supplied about two-thirds of the time, the question mark about half, while other marks were on the whole not used). Wilde also notes considerable variation between children ranging from 33.5% correct to 84.6% correct. There was also 'a dramatic improvement from third to fourth grade' according to Wilde. However, this is probably rather unfortunately phrased as the improvement is presumably from the average of the third grade to the average of the fourth. The one thing the data do not show clearly (although it could presumably have done so) is how the paths of the individual children gradually changed across time. Wilde only offers general comparisons for individual children across years. Her study was mainly about the spelling of the children and unfortunately she does not give the same attention to the punctuation. This is a pity because of all the studies noted it is the only one which has comprehensive data across a long time period.

It is worthwhile mentioning a couple of other studies which have something to say about beginning writers and punctuation. De Goes & Martlew (1983) report how, as part of a wider study of metacognition, they asked twenty children between 5.9 years and 6.8 years to copy a short piece of text which contained a variety of punctuation marks. They found that fewer than 50% copied the full stop or the comma. No children copied the ellipsis points. The most frequently reproduced marks were the question mark and the exclamation mark. Subsequent interviews indicated that most of the children did not know why the marks were different although many had a notion of 'ending' associated with the full stop. De Goes & Martlew suggest that the children, while copying, were dominated by the 'salient perceptual features'; in other words, the most letter-like punctuation marks were copied while the least letter-like marks (full stops and commas) were not (even though more children knew about their function). Unfortunately it is very difficult to know how to interpret these results. The Punctuation Project, led by the editors of this book, is carrying out a more detailed but similar study. What is clear already is that classroom experience makes a huge difference to what children notice as they copy and how they interpret the task (if it is set up as a handwriting exercise, then the nature of any previous handwriting experiences become significant in determining how a child decides what it is that needs to be copied). We have found, within the same school, a young class (and children were, on the whole, younger than those studied by De Goes & Martlew) who completely outperformed an older class on a copying task involving punctuation. It is certainly not simply age and saliency which makes the difference.

Calkins (1980) compared the ways in which children in two third-grade classrooms were able to talk about and define uses for punctuation marks. One teachers used a 'process writing' approach (Graves, 1983) in which children were enabled to write freely and where meaning was the central component of the writing experience (as was the case in Giacobbe's classroom — see above). In the other class, writing was taught more formally and involved 'language mechanics through daily drills and work book exercises'. In the subsequent interviews the 'process writers' were able to identify and explain an average of 8.66 kinds of punctuation while the children in the more formal class could only identify and explain 3.85 kinds. When the children in the formal class tried to explain they fell back on trying to remember the rules they had been taught. The other class referred to how they had used them in their writing to create particular effects. While most of the children in the 'process' classroom found punctuation interesting or enjoyable, only twenty-five percent of those in the formal classroom did so. At the end of the year the 'process' class were using an average of five kinds of punctuation per piece of writing.

Conclusion

I have dealt in some detail with these studies because they are the only ones which have set out to illuminate beginning learners' attempts to make sense of punctuation. What is clear is that they do not add up to a terribly coherent perspective on how beginners approach punctuation. This is not a criticism of any of the studies and if I have, in places, pointed out things that were not done in those studies it is not to see them negatively but simply to explore what has been covered and what has not. Indeed, we should be grateful that these studies have been done and wonder why many others have not taken their work onwards. It is worth summarising what those studies do tell us and what they do not.

The first point to make is that with the exception of the relationship between the studies involving Cordiero, they are all unrelated pieces of work; in other words they do not seem to have informed each other except in very general ways. No study sets out to test any other study. Thus, there is no clear sense of knowledge being taken forward by developing a theory or devising tests of a theory. Individually they might be related to more general theories but as a collection, the strongest thing one can say is that we have a bundle of intriguing facts, observations and suggestions. This bundle is an interesting one and there are some points about which there seems to be agreement.

All the authors suggest that learning to punctuate is not a passive process in which children simply learn a set of rules and can then punctuate accurately. Indeed, the class examined by Calkins (1980) which did have this kind of experience was not as effective with punctuation as the class which didn't. For all the authors, the child is actively constructing a view of how the punctuation system works. There is both system and direction in children's understanding of punctuation. Cordiero, Giacobbe & Cazden (1983) write about 'the hypotheses young children try to act upon', Edelsky (1983) writes that, 'Children's writing seemed to develop through internal and individual process of hypothesis creating/testing and schema development tapping', Ferreiro & Teberosky (1983) explain that 'what appears as confusion is actually the child's systematization, operating from bases very different from the adult's', and Kress (1982) in an analysis of one child's texts suggests that 'The child may be searching for a unit which can express some unified coherent concept which the child needs to express'.

It is also the case that the above studies suggest that change does take place, even in those classrooms in which there is little or no formal instruction in punctuation. Several of the studies suggest strongly that the move is towards understanding punctuation as a linguistic feature rather than as a graphic feature, which is where many of the studies suggest it begins. However, the studies also show that achieving understanding of the punctuation system is something which takes quite a long time; it is a slow process because punctuation is a complex object.

Despite that measure of agreement, and the effort of those researchers, there is much left unsaid. The first thing to say is that there is
no clear pattern of how knowledge of punctuation as a whole emerges.
The discreteness of the studies cannot be overcome by adding the bits
together; it does not make a coherent whole. Too few of the studies took
a developmental perspective and those that did were either for relatively
short periods of time or did not report the data in a developmental way.
Is there any relationship between the pre-school developments noted by
Ferreiro & Teberosky and the more advanced notions of Kress? What
happens as children move between the ages of four and eight and
beyond? There is still no long-term examination of how children make
sense of the meanings and uses of punctuation. Most important of all,
how do children actually move in the transitions from one kind of use
of punctuation to another; none of the studies looks in detail at how
these moves are made.

In almost all cases the examination of the children's behaviour was
essentially text-based rather than action-based. Thus relatively little, if any,
data were collected about the behaviour of children as they were actually
working in classrooms. Indeed, to a large extent the children themselves
seem missing from most of these studies. Children have voices and have
views about what they do in classrooms. Very few of the above studies
report in any significant way on the children's declared perspectives. There
is a great deal of assumption based upon textual analysis rather than talking
to children.

Equally, none of the studies either looked at, or reported in any
significant way on, the ecology of learning punctuation, despite most of
the authors acknowledging in some way that this is important. Children
in a classroom are learning about topics from many sources, at many
different times of the day, and in many different kinds of contexts. None
of the studies paid any serious attention to how the children made sense
of their learning within the complexity of classroom life. A few visits
and a couple of descriptions do not add up to an analysis of learning in
classrooms. Yet this is, undoubtedly, where much learning does go on
and where children meet many of their sources for learning. One
consequence of this is that virtually none of the studies make any
mention at all of the children's reading experiences. Punctuation is seen
almost exclusively as a problem of becoming a writer. To some extent
this is understandable; in the British National Curriculum, for example,
it is within writing that assessment of punctuation ability is placed, and
equally it is within writing that children's usage of punctuation is most
manifested. However, to ignore reading both as a source of information

about punctuation and as a process which might require knowledge about punctuation seems unfortunate (for instance Eckhoff, 1986, suggested that children engage in end-of-line punctuation because so much of the material they read is punctuated like that).

The above studies clearly do not represent the last word in understanding how punctuation is learnt. None of authors is any way suggesting that it is. Indeed, I suspect that many of them have wondered why the world of literary investigators appears not to have explored any further. It is certainly not for want of areas to be looked at. It would be very welcome to have studies which investigate:

- the development of knowledge about punctuation over extended periods of time. It would also be helpful to have such studies carried out in different environments, cultures and conditions.
- the ecology of learning punctuation and which really explore the ways in which learning to punctuate occurs within the all the complexities of classroom life.
- the true significance and status of punctuation in the lives of beginning readers and writers of all ages. For instance, my own observations suggest that it is a long time before children who know about punctuation actually put it in as they write. Most beginners seem go back after writing and seek out where to place it. When does punctuation cease to be something you put in because the teacher tells you to and become something you use to make your meaning clear?
- the relationships between classroom experiences and learning about punctuation and explore the kinds of conditions which are effective in encouraging the most efficient learning about punctuation.
- how knowledge of other punctuation marks develops and of the interrelationship between knowledge about different types of punctuation mark.
- how different kinds of learners cope with making sense of punctuation (see the chapter by Ruiz in this volume)
- the role of punctuation in reading and its relationship to knowledge about punctuation when writing.
- whether experience of different kinds of texts has any influence on children's use and knowledge of punctuation.
- how punctuation is learned in those written languages which use different punctuation conventions.

and, maybe, historians could even help us understand how punctuation has been taught in the past.

I started this chapter by suggesting that it could be a very short chapter. It has turned out to be quite a long one. This is because of the issues needing to be discussed rather than because there is a rich research literature documenting how people learn about punctuation. What is clear is that there are as many interesting questions about punctuation development as there are about any other area of language development. It is simply that, so far, no-one has answered them.

2 Invented Punctuation

PRISCA MARTENS and YETTA GOODMAN

Introduction

Punctuation is the conventionalised means by which an author shares with a reader necessary information about meaning or language structure not contained in the words of the text. Grammatical divisions such as sentences, clauses, phrases and words, along with marks signifying meaning, such as exclamations, support, clarify and enhance written messages for the reader.

While the punctuation system serves an important and vital function, it is not without weaknesses. Even children like Bill (see Example 2.1) are, from an early age, able to appreciate its limitations.

Bill is a third grader whose dog was killed. When writing about that tragedy in his life, he realised that while conventional punctuation indicates excitement with exclamation points, it has no means of adequately expressing sadness, such as he felt at the loss of his dog. So, as a remedy, he invented the 'Sadlamation' point (Goodman, 1979). Even Bill's 'Sadlamation' point, however, does not fully represent his emotions, the look in his eyes, the sound of his voice, or the emptiness and pain he was experiencing without his dog.

Our goal in this chapter is to demonstrate that children, like Bill, recognise the complexity of the relationship between oral and written language as they explore how punctuation can serve functional purposes in their writing. Their writing samples illustrate how they generate punctuation as a means of representing meanings that are not easily written in words and how they segment their written language to make it readable to others.

Difficulties arise for children such as Bill if they are taught a frequently accepted belief that a one-to-one relationship exists between oral and written language. It is not uncommon, for example, to hear written language described as 'speech written down'. In this definition, written

Dr Yetta Goodman,

I've invented a new punctuation mark. A mark for something sad. It is used in a sentence like this I had a dog, it died ↓ It does look funny, but it will get better looking soon, just like all of the others.

Mrs North's student.
Bill Patton

Example 2.1 Bill's 'Sadlamation' point

punctuation necessarily represents in an isomorphic way the intonation patterns of speech, thus alleviating the need for Bill's 'Sadlamation' point. Too often children are simply told to 'listen' for punctuation, placing commas where they pause, full stops where they stop, and exclamation points at the end of exciting sentences; yet such a set of instructions can be a recipe for confusion and failure.

Both oral and written language are generative language processes vital to our communication. They draw on the same systems of personal-social meanings to suit the situation and audience, and share a common vocabulary and many language structures. Despite these similarities, they also differ in significant ways. Oral language uses a cyclical and recursive stream of sound and has time as its major dimension. Topics are reintroduced for further discussion and elaboration, providing the speaker with immediate oral or visual feedback from the listener. Written language, on the other hand, uses visual input through symbols or characters in flat two-dimensional space. It is more organised with the writer usually completing one topic before moving to the next. Written texts are more durable and may be reviewed, reconstructed, and polished before they are read by the intended audience (K. Goodman, 1993).

Imagine, for example, a child describing to her mother the happenings of a day at school. Her complex sentences ramble on and on, but her intonation clarifies many of the structural ambiguities: her pitch, stress, juncture, and intonation segment her language into units of meaning and her voice quality, facial expression, body movements, voice speed, and volume express her feelings and emotions. Her mother is able to ask her immediately for elaboration or clarification about the day.

If the child was to write about the day in a letter to her grandparents, many things would change. Writing requires a different use of language. The fact that her grandparents are not visible and that her letter is the sole representation of her meanings, poses a different set of problems, necessitating a different organisation of language. The syntactic rules and the sentence structure change in order for her text to be comprehensible. She segments her language with spaces between words, paragraphs, capitals, full stops, etc., and any attempt to convey her feelings and emotions will require less frequently used graphic devices such as emboldening print, underlining, oversizing letters or words, or using colour and pictures. What the child is discovering is that written language is not usually as flexible as oral language (and this is especially true for young learners):

> Subtle shifts in the intonation of oral language may clarify what would be ambiguous statements in writing. That's because punctuation is not nearly so full and flexible a system for creating the patterns of written language. A written English sentence starts with a capital and ends with a period, question mark, or exclamation point. But it has nothing corresponding to the oral English sentence's intonational contour which marks it as a statement, question or command from beginning to end. Written English employs a variety of means such as underlining, boldface, italics, and oversize letters to indicate where special stress is in the text. None of these work quite as well as intonation in oral language. Only the exclamation point in written language gives any sense of the emotional state of a writer. (K. Goodman, 1994)

Anyone attempting to transcribe speech from an audio tape experiences firsthand the difficulties and frustrations that arise in transforming the power, liveliness, and emotion of oral language into cohesive and readable written language. Punctuating through segmentation and specific marks pales in comparison to the intonation and voice quality of oral language.

Apart from being limited in its ability to represent spoken language, punctuation is certainly not self-evident to a young writer. As children write and read they become aware of the existence of punctuation marks, but being 'aware' can be far from understanding the rules which govern their use. As with any rule-based system which is complicated to explain, children develop their knowledge of punctuation through a variety of processes and experiences. As they do so they face many problems for which there are either no easy answers. Children then do what all learners do. They invent solutions, drawing on all the knowledge and under-standing they have amassed through their growing experiences with written language in their environment. These inventions drive their learning and are constrained by societal conventions.

> I see children constructing their understandings of the world and their own responses to it in the context of the culture they belong to. And I see them as actively inventing language as they need it, but doing so in the context of the language of their home and community... The dynamic dialectic between personal invention and social convention is the dominant force in language and literacy development, as it is in all learning. (K. Goodman, 1993: 82–83)

We are well aware that for some the term *invention* causes consternation. However, by avoiding the inventive powers of young children, and all learners, we lack appreciation for their learning capacity and fail to acknowledge the learning process itself. As Piaget (1970) states:

> The problem we must solve, in order to explain cognitive development, is that of invention and not mere copying...the concepts of assimilation and accommodation of all operational structures (which are created, not merely discovered, as a result of the subject's activities), are oriented towards this inventive construction which characterises all living thought... *Remember also that each time one prematurely teaches a child something he could have discovered for himself, that child is kept from inventing it and consequently from understanding it completely* (italics added). (pp. 712–715)

Our research on early literacy development supports Piaget's notions of invention. It verifies that children who are immersed in a rich, supportive literacy environment at home and school write very naturally. As they perceive reasons to write, be it for buying food, keeping in touch with friends or providing information, they invent and adapt forms to frame those functions. Over time, the necessity of a means to clarify their writing for their readers becomes clear and they start to appreciate the reasons for the punctuation they see in written language. Drawing on their background knowledge and experiences, they generate hypotheses for when and how punctuation functions and incorporate punctuation into their own writing to represent meaning and segment written language into units, just as they see it doing in conventional writing systems. Children's use of punctuation may not always be conventional but it is evidence of their developing understanding that our written language system requires special markings to serve its unique functions.

Only in environments where children are free to be risk-takers and explore language use are such problem-solving solutions fostered. When children are not afraid of writing then they are as thoughtfully creative in their exploration of punctuation as they were with their earlier use of spoken language, and as they are in their discoveries about the ways in which spelling works. The children whose writings we now examine live in homes and classrooms supportive of their explorations and discoveries about literacy and punctuation.

Punctuation that Represents Meaning

As the needs arise, children explore ways to represent their meanings, some of which may extend beyond the boundaries of what is normally thought of as punctuation. This is particularly true where the emotions are concerned. Emotion and feelings, whether excitement, boredom, anger, sadness, or worry, are a natural part of our humanness which constantly permeates our oral language. Through our volume, voice speed, and facial expression, for example, we emphasise the personal and emotional importance of the meanings we are expressing.

Written language is constrained to expressing meaning through exclamation points, font differences and capital letters at the beginning of sentences, for proper names and titles. Bill's recognition of such constraints in written language prompted his Sadlamation point (see Example 2.1). The need and desire to represent and convey personal meanings in written language is common to all of us and a strong impetus for children to create new punctuation devices.

Shoshana, age 8, was making a Mother's Day card as a surprise for her mother. To highlight the love the card represented, Shoshana invented special punctuation to fulfil her meaning and purpose. Her stars, setting apart her 'Sipprys' (surprise) and her hearts with dots underneath approximating exclamation points, emphasise and represent her love. Recognising this was new and unfamiliar punctuation to her mother, Shoshana even invented a key in the lower right hand corner for clarification: 'The heart stands for loud!' (see Example 2.2).

Exclamation points and invented punctuation like Shoshana's efficiently serve the dual role of segmenting text and representing meaning.

Example 2.2 Shoshana's 'heart' punctuation

Jack and Dorsey, seventh graders, were writing rap. Because rap is spoken in a rhythm with certain phrases louder or faster than others, they wanted to punctuate their raps so readers would know how to appropriately read them. Not knowing musical notations, these two composers invented a punctuation so as to share their interpretations with their readers. Jack's concern was volume (see Example 2.3). So, his punctuation, _____/, indicates where to rap more loudly.

You know what'll happen If I go at this rate.
My Mother will turn me into a can of Fish bate.
You know I tryingtobe'cool, trying to play by the
rules.
But that's how I survive on the first day of
schod.

Example 2.3 Jack's punctuation to indicate an increase in volume

Mrs. Curry always like her room real clean
If it aint she'll let of steam!
There's current events that are due and theirs
no accuse for the News, interviews, or debues.
If you dont do that youll' melt in shoes
Now thats the end of my delirias rap
Always remember "Honey Don't play Dat.

Example 2.4 Dorsey's punctuation for speed

Dorsey's concern, on the other hand, was speed at a specific point in his rap (see Example 2.4). His arrows provide directions for where the rapper needs to read faster.

Even very young children invent punctuation for meaning. Julio, age 4, wanted to write a note to surprise his neighbour Ana (see Example 2.5). Ana was using the mail box to write to Julio's older sister, an experience in which Julio wanted to participate. So, he invented rebus writing using conventional punctuation forms to represent his meaning for Ana. Even through she knew the intention of Julio's writing, Ana still asked him to read what he wrote. He replied, 'It says "To Ana From Guess Who? Julio".' Somewhat insecure about Ana understanding his punctuation, Julio explained that the reversed question mark represented 'Guess Who?' and the equals sign, with the arrow going in both directions, represented 'from'.

TOANA!⇆JULIO

Example 2.5 Julio's 'Guess who?'

Just as the boundary lines between other aspects of language are not always clear and neat, neither are the lines defining punctuation. To help bridge the gap between oral and written language and to make authors' personal written meanings more explicit and understandable for their readers, human beings as a culture have invented and accepted certain ways of representing meanings which are not commonly thought of as punctuation. If an exclamation mark and a question mark can be punctuation, then a strong case could be made out for the use of many other graphic devices to be considered part of the punctuation system of language.

Graphic features such as oversized letters, underlining, and XOXO for kisses and hugs punctuate meaning and emphasis in written language. Children see these graphic features in notes, advertisements, environmental print, or greeting cards, and invent their own uses of them very early. They may even see some in their early reading books! Trevi's happy face heart in her memo to her dad (see Example 2.6) punctuates emphasis and feeling into her expression of love. She could call it a 'love point' in the same way that Bill named his 'Sadlamation' point.

Example 2.6 Trevi's memo

Example 2.7 Tracey's story

One of the commonest means of indicating emphasis is to use colour, size, or typeface. Tracey, age five used just such a form of punctuation when she wanted her reader to know just how scary the dark wood was (see Example 2.7). She could do this easily when reading her story aloud, but how was she to represent this in her writing? Her answer was 'size'.

Lest readers think that such creative responses lie outside the scope of a book on punctuation, they might like to know that many times during the last four hundred years people have invented, and tried to impose punctuation marks which extend the function of our most conventional marks. John Wilkins writing in his 'Essay towards a real character, and philosophical language' (1668) said about indicating 'irony':

> For if the chief force of ironies do consist in pronunciation, it will plainly follow, that there ought to be some mark for direction, when things are to be so pronounced. (p. 329)

Thus, children are not alone in wanting to find marks to express things not easily rendered by 'normal' punctuation. These can all be categorised as punctuation; part of the non-alphabetic writing system serving as support to the alphabetic writing system.

Punctuation that Segments Written Language

We understand continuous streams of words in oral language because of the clarification provided by factors such as intonation, pitch, pause, stress, juncture, situational context, and movement. Written language relies more on spacing, paragraphing, and a whole range of conventional punctuation marks for clarification. Thus, punctuation serves the writer's purpose of clarifying meaning for the reader. Children's use of segmentation suggests their awareness that what they write will have an audience.

It took centuries of use for written language systems to use segmentation in a consistent manner. Spacing and final sentence punctuation did not enter English until the 1100s. Commas and quotation marks are even more recent inventions. Children experience a process similar to the earliest inventors of punctuation as they create ways of segmenting their written language. Before learning written conventions, it is not at all uncommon for young beginning writers to run all of their words and sentences together in one long string, similar to writing centuries ago. Because they do not 'hear' spaces between words in speech, they do not initially incorporate space as a segmenting signal into their writing. Their writing 'looks' like the continuous stream of sound they hear. As their immersion in written language continues through rich experiences at home and school, being read to, observing others write, experimenting themselves with writing, and becoming aware that unpunctuated text can be ambiguous, their utilisation of written segmentation grows. At first, they do not understand the social conventions of spacing between words, phrasal and clausal groupings marking ends of sentences, and grouping sentences into paragraphs to support and clarify their meanings, and so they invent ways to incorporate segmentation into their writing.

For example, Terri, age 6 (see Example 2.8) was becoming aware of spacing between words and sentences, with the space between sentences differing from that between words. She invented a means of separating her words, indicating where sentences begin and end to support her reader's comprehension. Her '+' between each word in a sentence and '-' between sentences are overt evidence of her intuitive awareness of the difference in these segmentation units, and in her growing competence in knowing the concepts of 'wordness' and 'sentenceness'. Her developing understanding of conventional punctuation is visible in the full stops she also inserts at the end of some sentences.

Robert, at an earlier age (5 years 1 month), used a dot to segment his words even when his words consisted of no more than the initial letter sounds representing a word or syllable (see Example 2.9).

Terri

Wetwa ch et+f oo+ba\\+ast nite-And +we+went+to+the foo+ba\\+gam e+the+n ite bfor+that +n ite+we+wachet foo+ba\\.-a nd+that+too k+tw oweres -ther +was+foo+ball to+l a s t.-

Example 2.8 Terri's representation of segmentation

h ·f· W·D·f ·P· L·P· b ·n·P

Example 2.9 Robert's story (trans. An fire engine with a fire and lots of people and an dog)

Robert and Terri, in using a mark to segment words, are simply doing what Roman stone masons often did when they chiselled texts onto stone.

Children also invent other ways to segment written language as illustrated in the dinosaur story in Example 2.10, authored by Marie, a five-year-old kindergarten child. Marie knew that full stops marked the end of a story and told her teacher she put a full stop there to signal 'The end'.

Wos   Then   WAZ   a   ᴅAᴧSoᴋ
Aᴧᵶd   The   ᴅAᴧSoᴋ   LaP   a
Eᵉeag.   ᴧ   Then   The   PAᴧSoᴦ
WaT   a   WaE.   ᴧ   Then
a   Maᴧ   Foᴧᴅ   The
eeag   aᴧᴅ   TEC   The
ᴅAᴧSoᴦ   eeag   To   a   Muzaᴧ.

Example 2.10 A kindergarten child's breath marks

That she is also developing a concept of sentence is evident in her 'breath marks'. After Marie read her story to her teacher, the teacher asked what those marks were since Marie made no reference to them as she read. Marie responded, 'I knew you would read my story to the other kids so I put those marks there so you'd know where to take some breaths.'

Punctuating with full stops, commas, or question marks segments written language by indicating sentence, clause or phrase boundaries. While these marks do separate units of language, they go much further and also indicate grammatical relationships between those units. The relationship between two units separated by a comma is different from the relationship established by a full stop or a semi-colon. Most children have few problems with learning to put space between words to separate them from each other, but it does take them a few years into their schooling to establish the nature and function of the more complex forms of conventional punctuation.

As children's experience with written language grows, and as they talk to people about written language, so their awareness of these more complicated conventions increases. However, the rules governing the use of these marks are not easily explained or intuited, and children invent hypotheses to account for usage. Often this involves an over-generalisation, such as placing the punctuation mark frequently and unconventionally. Continued experience with writing, reading, and talking about their inventions with understanding teachers and parents supports children in refining their understandings.

Many children punctuate first by spacing between words. Sarah, age 4, like Robert began with full stops, but whereas Robert was using them simply as a device to create space, Sarah became aware of their function of

deR KABI   Y VAK   U 1
Dear Grandpa, Thank you fo-

R_ V Kd Ad BZL.
r the candy and puzzle.

I L   U   SARAH
I love you   Sarah

Example 2.11 Sarah's use of full stops

marking 'the end' or 'stop' of a unit of meaning. She did this through seeing them in books and in her environment, and hearing them discussed by her parents and older brother. Perceiving full stops as a convention of written language to segment units of meaning, she began consistently incorporating them into her writing. Example 2.11 shows a letter Sarah wrote to her grandfather.

Sarah does not always place her full stops conventionally, but she

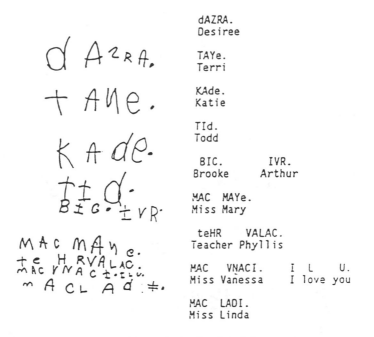

dAZRA.
Desiree

TAYe.
Terri

KAde.
Katie

TId.
Todd

BIC.   IVR.
Brooke   Arthur

MAC MAYe.
Miss Mary

teHR   VALAC.
Teacher Phyllis

MAC VNACI.   I L   U.
Miss Vanessa   I love you

MAC LADI.
Miss Linda

Example 2.12 Sarah's list of friends for her birthday party demonstrates developing understanding of their function in written language and successfully uses them to separate distinct units of sense. Sarah's full stops also appeared in other writing. Example 2.12 is a list of friends she wanted to invite to her birthday party.

Here, Sarah places full stops to mark the end of each name. While this is not often a conventional function of full stops (although it is a typical use of a semi-colon) it shows that Sarah is aware that full stops mark the end of units of thought; she is developing the concept of sentenceness.

Commas, apostrophes, hyphens, and other segmentation conventions take time to conceptualise and learn to control. English orthography uses commas to segment grammatical units such as clauses, phrases including a series, and in language units such as dates, letters, and geographical locations. Hyphens relate to spelling and line spacing; apostrophes relate to both spelling, as in contractions, and grammar, as in possessives. Deciding which to use when and where is often complex, as Matthew demonstrates in his letter in Example 2.13.

When Matthew, age 8, got in trouble at camp for misbehaving, his parents suggested he write a letter of apology to his counsellor. Knowing

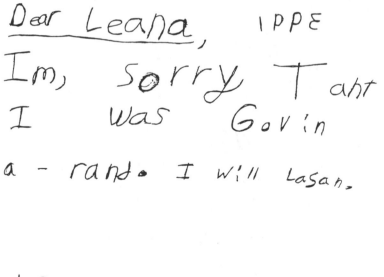

Example 2.13 Matthew's apology letter

a comma is used in both the salutation and closing, he placed it after his name in the closing since it goes after the name in the salutation. For added emphasis, he underlined them both. Matthew is also aware that 'I'm' requires some kind of mark. Because the same mark is positioned differently, depending on whether it is a comma, apostrophe, or quotation mark, Matthew over-generalises again and invents a form with the comma after 'I'm' instead of the needed apostrophe. He also hyphenates, correctly but unnecessarily, a two syllable word. His responses demonstrate intelligent assumptions about how linguistic rules might extend in novel situations.

Nine-year-old C.C. is obviously thinking hard about when and when not to insert an apostrophe before an 's' (and when he needs full stops).

Example 2.14 contains C.C.'s announcement, in a sports reporter's style, of Super Bowl 12. His hypothesis on the use of apostrophes at this point in time is to insert them before a final 's' on short words of four letters or less.

> Super Bowl 12
>
> Denver vs Dallas
> Denver wins the filp and D.D. Lewis
> and fombles at the 45 and Danny
> White recavers and get's to
> the 57 it first and 10⁹ Danny
> White pass to Ionny Dorset get's
> to the 32 it's 1 and 3 and
> Dorset get's 36 for a 3 and 2.
> And Danny White kik's a
> field gold 3-0 Dallas
> 2 Quriter
>
> It's 3 Quriter
> And Otis armstrong get's to
> the 57 and he fombles and
> Craig Morton take's it in for a
> T. D. And Denver won 7-3
>
> by C.C.

Example 2.14 C.C.'s use of apostrophes

Of the nine times he applied his hypothesis, only two, both 'it's', were conventional and not an over-generalisation of present tense verbs ending in 's'. And, on two other occasions (one for the contraction 'it's' and one the possessive 'White's') he did not use apostrophe 's' when it was conventional to do so. It is interesting to notice that C.C. does not use the apostrophe when the final 's' is on longer words ('fumbles' or 'recovers') or on proper nouns ('Dallas' or' Otis'). He over-generalises in specific and appropriate contexts.

As with all language inventions and conventions that young writers face, the complexity of the language poses many challenges but given opportunities to write for many functions and purposes, and appreciation for their intelligent hypotheses which they will work with and adapt until they shift to more conventional uses of punctuation, young writers continue hypothesising and solving their problems.

Conclusion

The writing samples we examined above clearly provide evidence that children understand what some adults do not: oral and written language do not have an isomorphic relationship. Punctuation is a feature of written language functioning independently from oral language which a writer employs to clarify meanings for the reader. Moreover, it is simply not possible to take oral meanings, feelings, and emotions and convey them directly in written language.

The samples also show that children do not use punctuation in a passive way. Their inventions illuminate their developing knowledge and understanding of the rules, and all the situations where they might or might not apply. They are actively responding to the rules they know and testing them out in many different situations. In the process they show us how much they know, not how little!

When children discover written language can be ambiguous for readers and not represent their meanings strongly enough, they clarify by inventing punctuation to serve their purposes. In doing so they demonstrate an understanding of the nature and purpose of punctuation that should never be contradicted by endless worksheets purely for the sake of drill. Such exercises, far from clarifying concepts of punctuation, are more likely to engender confusion as they replace sense by imposing routine in a totally decontextualised manner.

Parents, teachers, and developers of workbook exercises and test items must become more knowledgeable about the ways children understand punctuation. Including artificial comma exercises for first graders or quotation mark items for second graders in tests or workbooks is absolutely contrary to what teachers and researchers are discovering about the punctuation development of young children.

For children's understandings of punctuation to develop they need time, many experiences and opportunities, and support as they are immersed in reading and writing rich, authentic, functional language. By learning to read as a writer they observe how authors use different features of punctuation in different contexts, both in connected discourse and in other print environments. Using Big Books or small group reading time to focus on how authors use punctuation is a way of helping kids read like a writer. By taking advantage of such teachable moments and with appropriately planned short informal lessons in relation to student's authentic reading and writing experiences, teachers heighten children's awareness in a purposeful meaningful context of when and how specific punctuation is used. In editing their own writing of notes, letters, stories, reports, and posters for authentic purposes children draw on and apply their growing understandings. Their inventions and over-generalisations of punctuation demonstrate their developing conceptualisation of how the written language system works.

Only through being continually supported in their exploration and invention of written language as readers, recognising punctuation in literature, the environment, and the writing of others, and as authors creating, organising, and controlling their own writing, will children refine and strengthen their understanding and control of these meaningful written language conventions.

3 Vicki's Story: A Seven-year-old's Use and Understanding of Punctuation

HOLLY ANDERSON

Introduction

I became acquainted with Vicki when, as an Advisory Teacher for English, I spent some time working with her teacher and the class of, what were then, Year One children (age five and six). We were sharing books together and I had noticed how competent Vicki seemed to be. She read expressively and with obvious enjoyment. There was something in her manner, a thoughtful, reflective quality, which made me feel she appreciated not just the storyline but also the way in which the author had crafted the book. We began to discuss how books are written and published, the vocabulary chosen and the layout of the pages. I had not at that time considered mentioning punctuation and was surprised when Vicki pointed to a colon and said she thought (correctly) that it indicated the next few words would be a list of things. We therefore moved into a discussion about the marks on the pages and their functions, which Vicki seemed to be aware of without being able to name them. She was unable to offer an explanation for her knowledge and this increased my fascination.

How much understanding do young children have of punctuation marks? How do they distinguish between letters and punctuation? What do they read? What do they ignore? Most importantly, how do they develop their understanding? Vicki did not seem to have been taught, nor could she recollect having ever discussed punctuation with anyone before. Was she unusual or, given the opportunity, would other children show a similar awareness?

At the time I did not pursue this further, but merely stored it away as another area in which children challenge our assumptions and show that they are often more capable than we realise. However, in the light of England's new National Curriculum requirements, I thought back to Vicki. Every child in England is now, at around the age of seven, assessed in a number of areas by doing what are called Standard Assessment Tasks (or SATs). In English, punctuation is one of the areas examined. The children are asked to undertake a piece of writing and the extent to which they have used punctuation, and used it correctly, forms part of their overall assessment (for more detailed information see Chapter 5).

As Vicki had seemed to know about a variety of punctuation marks, how had she used them in her SATs writing task? How had other children fared? Was use of punctuation a clear indication of writing development? I decided to investigate this further. I taped informal interviews with 17 late six- or seven-year-old children drawn from four different schools, all having just taken SATs. The children read the writing they had done for this assessment, read a book of their own choice and talked with me about the punctuation marks in both. This gave me an opportunity to see whether they used punctuation when reading aloud as well as whether they could name punctuation marks and/or describe their functions. In addition I analysed the sentence structure in their pieces of writing to see what other features could be seen in their development as writers.

Although, perhaps inevitably, more questions have been raised than answered, Vicki's story challenged me as an educator to reflect on children's ability to notice punctuation and make hypotheses about its functions. In this chapter I report on my time observing Vicki's use of, and listening to her talk about, punctuation. However, it is important to place her behaviour in a wider context so I will compare her behaviour with that of some of the other children.

Reading

It was noticeable that even though the text (from both reading schemes — basal readers — and 'real' books) ranged from single sentences on the page to a number of sentences, most pages could be read without needing to make use of the punctuation. The meaning was firmly embedded within the vocabulary and syntax of the text, and there were few sentences which would need careful attention to punctuation for clarity. Layout too, with clause breaks often coinciding with the end of lines, also enabled children to pause at meaningful breaks in the text, giving an impression of fluency without having to be dependent on punctuation for interpretation. Authors of books for young children and editors of reading schemes presumably want to minimise the amount of information a child has to use in order to be successful, but this meant that it was difficult to decide whether or not children were, in fact, paying attention to punctuation. Only three children, including Vicki, chose books which did require closer attention to punctuation and she was the only one to demonstrate that punctuation was one of the features of the text to be taken into account.

One boy appeared to ignore the punctuation in his text, finishing sentences at the end of a line where, in fact, a comma should have indicated a continuation. He also misread words in order to maintain the meaning he had constructed. The text reads:

(1) At last he came out of the wood,
(2) and saw Simon's house.
(3) He ran to the door.
(4) 'Let me in! Let me in!' he cried
(5) as he knocked. 'All the animals...

Although it is difficult to be absolutely sure, it seems, from noting the pauses and the word substitutions, that he read the text as if it were:

(1) At last he came out of the wood.
(2) He saw Simon's house
(3) and ran to the door.
(4) 'Let me in! Let me in!' he cried.
(5) As he knocked all the animals...

After he had indicated through his intonation that 'wood' in the first line was the end of a sentence, he was caught out when starting the second line. He clearly realised that few sentences do start with 'and', but instead of re-reading the first line, altered the second line. Similarly, having ignored the full stop at the end of line 2, he continued the sentence on to the next line and so had to link the clauses in some way. This time he replaced 'He' by 'and'. The need to link a line break to a sentence break appeared to be very strong (and most of the books read by the children supported this) and he again read the end of line 4 as if it were the end of a sentence. Thus, he had to read line 5 as if it were a new sentence which started with an adverbial clause (a common feature in written English).

The sentence break in the middle of line 5, probably the most difficult of all as it does not coincide with a line break, was ignored and the two clauses were joined together. However, throughout his reading of the text he read fluently and with expression, keeping a plausible, if not always accurate, sentence construction (for more information about the children's reading of direct speech see the chapter by Perera in this book).

Vicki, however, indicated through her intonation that she may have been using punctuation as one of her strategies. Whilst I cannot be certain of this, she was the only child in the study to show she might have taken punctuation into account. The text reads:

(1) Mum put the brake on the push-chair and
(2) left Annie Rose at the bottom of the steps
(3) while she lifted the basket of shopping up to
(4) the top. Then she found the key…

Vicki paused almost imperceptibly at the end of line 2, perhaps checking to see whether it was the end of the sentence, which syntactically was possible. However the adverbial clause 'while she lifted the basket' at the beginning of line 3 does not start a new sentence but refers to the previous noun phrase, and Vicki continued to read down the four lines without breaking the sentence before finally pausing (correctly) at the full stop in the middle of line four. Whether Vicki was influenced by the punctuation marks is hard to prove. All that can be said is that she read the extract with expression consistent with the punctuation in the text, seeming to take notice of exclamation marks, question marks and speech marks as well as pausing and raising and dropping tone in appropriately different ways when confronted by a full stop or a comma. The subsequent conversation, transcribed below, also indicates that she was aware of the functions of the different punctuation marks.

H: Are there things that help you decide how to read?
V: There are speech marks. And those, I've forgotten what they're called.
H: They're called exclamation marks. Do you know what they're for?
V: They're for if someone is shouting, or excited, or something like that. That's what they're for…
H: Is there any other punctuation that you've noticed?
V: Commas. (Pointing to an apostrophe in 'didn't')…
H: That's called an apostrophe. Do you know what they're for?
V: If you've left a letter out to shorten a word, you'd put an apostrophe there to show you've left something out.
H: Yes, you do. What are full stops for?
V: They're the end of a sentence, it shows when you're starting a…when you've started to talk about something else.

In the same way that I had been impressed with Vicki's manner the previous year, I again found the way in which she thoughtfully reflected on her reading made me feel she did have some understanding of punctuation. In addition, her ability to articulate her thoughts gave me a deeper insight into these processes in a way in which was not possible with the other children. Whether this was an indication of a greater understanding is difficult to prove, but she was unique in being able to both demonstrate and articulate her perceptions. She seemed more aware of my needs as a listener and tried to define terms in ways which were not tautologous. For example, most of the children able to describe the function of a question mark would say it was to indicate a question (not an unreasonable definition in itself, but of little use to someone who might not understand the term 'question').

Child 'N':   You put a question mark because you want them to answer a question.

Similarly, with full stops:

Child 'A':   Yeah, I know where it's the end of a sentence or not.
Child 'F':   Because it was going on to a new sentence.

They knew that full stops had to be put at the end of a sentence, but were not able to explain how they had decided what constituted the end.

Vicki seemed to realise that she needed to define what a sentence was and so altered 'it shows when you're starting a...' (presumably sentence) to '...when you've started to talk about something else'. Did she take my needs into account? She certainly chose to end the reading of her chosen extract of text with all the skills of a soap opera editor, leaving me full of suspense and knowing just enough to want more.

As a speaker and reader there was a maturity which did not seem to be displayed to the same degree by the other children in the study and I wanted to see whether this was reflected in Vicki's ability as a writer.

Writing

In a three-page story written for SATs Vicki also demonstrated that she was capable of using a variety of techniques to keep a reader interested throughout the narrative. She used simple, compound and complex sentences structures (only one of two children in the study to use all three) as well as extended phrases, in her case adverbial. This was the most common type of extended phrase, used by five children in all, whereas noun phrases were used by two children (Vicki not being one). Apart from a change of tense from past to simple present, Vicki's syntax was consistent throughout a long and carefully constructed piece of writing which, although showing signs of slipping into a chronological recount, nevertheless contained some awareness of the tension and resolution required of narrative.

Apart from the handwriting being script rather than cursive, which, at the time, was school policy, and did not, therefore, reflect Vicki's inability in that area, her writing showed all the features necessary to be within Level 3 of the SATs (an above average level for a seven-year-old). Her use of punctuation more than met the demands of the National Curriculum. In addition to the compulsory demarcation of sentences (in Vicki's case by using both full stops and exclamation marks as well as capital letters) she used both a possessive and a missing letter apostrophe, brackets, and a hyphen. She also used a speech-bubble in her illustration to denote direct speech. However, in spite of such an impressive range (she used a larger variety of punctuation marks than any other child in the study), she was not consistent in her use. Sentences were not always started with capital letters, which were peppered throughout her writing (although never used in the middle of words), and were often left without a concluding punctuation mark. Even though there is evidence of her having re-read her work in order to correct errors (for example a small case 'o' in 'one' is altered at the beginning of a sentence), she was not able to self-correct throughout. The only two children in the whole study to sustain correct punctuation throughout their work each wrote only four or five sentences (all simple in construction). The punctuation in Vicki's longer and more complex piece of work was not able to be sustained in the same way.

Vicki's use of capital letters is interesting. She often used them to begin nouns; for example: Egg, World, Birthday, Breakfast, Lunch. She showed an awareness of the use of capitals in proper nouns (Little Walden Road, Dingy, Tink) and perhaps in these other words she was experimenting with an hypothesis she had formed. It seemed on analysis that they were not used at random as they were always at the beginning of words, often starting a sentence and, apart from three occasions, always to denote nouns.

Most of the children in the study seemed less aware of capital letters than the other sentence indicators. Although most used them at the beginning of some sentences (only two consistently), very few referred to capital letters when asked to talk about punctuation. On reflection, this may be due to the overlap of functions: letters are used to form words, and capital letters have a variety of purposes, not just sentence demarcation.

Vicki appeared to have more problems with use of capital letters than several of the other children who had merely omitted them at the beginnings of sentences. However, it is possible that she may have been at a more advanced stage which, although her work contained many errors, showed a greater awareness of the variety of functions. She demonstrated an ability to construct more complex sentences, another factor which may have had a bearing on the number of errors. Certainly another of the only two children to punctuate correctly throughout their work, may have been helped by the format she had chosen. She had drawn five pictures to illustrate sequences in a story, to which she then added five sentences as captions. Vicki's narrative provided a much richer and denser text, and a greater opportunity in which to experiment. Her use of punctuation was part of this experimentation.

Reading Their Own Writing

All the children read their stories to me as if they had used correct punctuation throughout. As when reading their chosen books aloud, in their own writing they seemed aware of the structure of written language and so read back their work as if written in complete, punctuated sentences. Even one of the poorer writers had an appreciation of this structure when 'reading' her work. The writing was a series of marks on the paper, several being straight, vertical lines, and showed neither sound–symbol correspondence nor letters grouped in an attempt to represent words. However she still 'read:

Father Christmas said one, one, one, one

presumably trying to make sense of the marks which did, in fact, look like numerals.

Vicki too read back her work as if correctly punctuated regardless of whether the sentences had been demarcated on the paper. In her piece of writing (see Example 3.1) she wrote:

First I make dingy's Breakfast then Dingy plays and I make him some new clothes. Wile he put his new clothes on I make his Lunch. Then we play together and Then we have diner. and put on Our night clothes.

However, when she read it aloud she ignored the first full stop and the subsequent capital letter, and joined an adverbial clause fronting the new sentence to the previous one.

First I make Dingy's breakfast then Dingy plays and I make him some new clothes while he puts his new clothes on

She immediately hesitated as if sensing something was not quite right, but then continued the story without going back to self-correct:

I make his lunch

Then she paused, as if checking meaning, and continued:

and then we play together and then we have dinner and put on our night clothes.

'that meens bye')

part 2

Because Dingy and Tink speak a diffreint Languege. They speak Juipist

Dingy's day

First I make dingy's Breakfast then Dingy plays and I make him some new clothes. Wile he put his new clothes on I make his Lunch. Then we play together and Then we have diner and put on our night clothes. I turn of the Lite and we snuggle down in our beds and thats what we are doing now snore snore snore snore snore.

Example 3.1

Even though most of her story was read with expression and as if punctuated throughout, Vicki was not consistent in her ability to use and describe punctuation. However, in the subsequent interview she showed that she had considered a variety of punctuation marks when writing, and once again it was her thoughtful reflective manner rather than the words she used which led me to feel she was aware of punctuation as a strategy which would help convey meaning through written language.

H: How did you decide where to put your full stops?
V: When I said 'One Summer day I was planting a seed and I came to a very hard bit of ground', I would put a full stop there because it's

the end of a sentence, otherwise it seems like 'I uncovered the prettiest egg in the world' is part of that sentence as well.

H: ...and when did you decide to use exclamation marks?

V: Lots of times when I put strange things happening, when I put the end bit I kept putting exclamation marks.

H: (pointing to a speech bubble in the illustration) If that had been part of your story, how would you have showed it was what the Ding Wing was saying?

V: I could have put that (*sic*) he was saying in speech marks.

H: (pointing to brackets by the speech bubble of the Ding Wing) What have you used there?

V: Brackets, because he was saying something and I had to put something extra otherwise people wouldn't know what it meant.

So Vicki was able to appreciate the need to interpret 'ging' (meaning 'bye-bye') for a non-Jupitese (her name for the Ding Wing language) speaking reader, and was able to use brackets to denote the aside. This added to my conviction that she had the needs of her readers clearly in mind when writing, and was able to discuss this awareness in a way which none of the other children in the study could. I was able to use her ability to articulate her thoughts to find out more about how she approached the writing process.

H: It looks as if you've actually done some alterations here. Why?

V: Because when I'd written it I read it through to make sure I had everything in the right place and I hadn't missed anything out, and I had a full stop there and I saw a little 'r' so I put a big one...

H: Do you find it difficult?

V: Well sometimes, it depends on how long the story is. If I do that much writing (indicates a few lines in her book) then it's easy because I just put, I just read it through quickly and put all my things there, but when it's a long story I'm not quite sure where all the full stops and things should go.

H: So do you find it difficult when you're doing your actual writing to remember to put in your punctuation?

V: If it's quick, about two sentences, I can do it fast, and if it's a very long story I can do it afterwards.

I was unable to find out from the other children about the range of approaches they used, but Vicki was clear that she found it more difficult to punctuate longer, more complicated pieces of writing as she went along. It may have been simply that they were not so able to explain the processes, but Vicki, as one of the most competent writers in the study, was able to describe her work as a writer, including her use of punctuation. I do not want to make any claims to a superior ability on her part, but instead to use what she enabled me to understand about her as a writer to reflect on issues raised by my observations.

Conclusion

On one hand, Vicki's use of a wide variety of punctuation marks reflected her range of other writing strategies and thus could be said to indicate her developmental stage. However, her written work was not consistently accurate, and if we are to measure achievement in terms of percentage of correctness, the other child's storyboard sequence was more successful in spite of not showing the depth or breadth of Vicki's less accurate piece.

However, if knowledge of punctuation is considered to be important, Vicki has more understanding than her writing would lead us to believe on first sight. It is only through looking at her language development in a wider context, by gaining knowledge of her as a reader and a speaker as well as writer, that a more honest picture can begin to emerge. Through close analysis and discussion, and the fact that Vicki was both articulate and thoughtful, this was made possible. However we need to approach such assessment with great caution as there is no real guarantee that a child less articulate than Vicki has, in fact, less understanding.

As teachers we may need to discuss punctuation in a wider context and to give more children the opportunities given to Vicki. However, perhaps more importantly, we also need to provide as many opportunities as possible to allow children to write for an audience and to discuss with them the need to make our intentions as writers more specific. Vicki was able to articulate this important aspect of awareness of reader; we have to ensure it is made explicit to all children. By allowing children to reflect on, and discuss, the way language is used both by them and around them we give them the possibility to extend and refine their hypotheses. Punctuation is one area to consider in this process and does need to be addressed.

However, to overemphasise correct use of punctuation at an age when many children in other European countries have yet to start school may have an adverse rather than a beneficial effect. With so much hanging on test scores and their publication, teachers may feel the need to play safe, and to encourage the children to write in ways which are more likely to be correctly punctuated. What would happen to Vicki if she felt unable to take risks and experiment with the hypotheses she had formed? What if she were discouraged to write within a complex structure? Do we not owe it to the children in our care to both support and challenge them in order to help them mature into more confident and dynamic writers?

4 Just Periods and Exclamation Points: The Continued Development of Children's Knowledge About Punctuation

SANDRA WILDE

Two comments from nine-year-old children about punctuation. Elaine, who used periods erratically and unconventionally, on one occasion said that she used them 'when there's a capital letter' and that she had used one in the middle of the abbreviation 'Ms.' (*m.s* in her rendition) because 'they always do.' Gordon wrote the sentence 'It was April the 13, 1982' with the numbers '13' and '1982' preceded by reversed commas and followed by normal ones. When asked why, he stated that his punctuation marks were commas and that they should be used in that unusual way when writing 'a month or a state.' Imagine the task that faces children learning to write who need to not only express their ideas in written form but also deal with conventions like spelling and the more difficult punctuation (which cannot, after all, be looked up in a dictionary). We know a small amount about young children's early emergent knowledge of punctuation (see Chapter 1 in this book), but such knowledge continues to develop as young writers construct more complex sentences and texts and continue to see additional uses of punctuation in their reading. Indeed, knowledge about punctuation is still developing in many adults, who may use marks such as the semicolon only rarely unless they are professional writers and who may (since they have perhaps never really understood what was taught to them about dependent and independent clauses) still be prone to producing fragments and run-on sentences.

As part of a larger study of the development of six children's knowledge about spelling and punctuation (Wilde, 1987), I examined their use of 1,254 punctuation marks across 215 texts, most of them narratives. Their use of punctuation illuminates some of the developmental patterns and issues that emerge as children grow beyond their initial knowledge base.

The children were studied over a period of two academic years during third and fourth grade in a public school in the United States, and were for the most part from eight- to nine-years-old at the time. The children were in three different classrooms during the two years of the study; all the classrooms provided regular time for writing, but none had the kind of writers' workshop focus described by Graves (1983), Calkins (1994), and others. What I will be describing here is not so much the influence of the classroom on punctuation development as what that development itself looked like in one particular setting.

Let us begin by getting a general sense of how well these six children used the four punctuation marks that occurred with any regularity in their writing. They were, in order of frequency, periods, commas, quotation marks, and question marks. Table 4.1 shows how often each of these was used appropriately, omitted, or used inappropriately. ('Appropriately' was defined as a reasonable standard of conventional punctuation.)

Table 4.1 Use of four punctuation marks across six children

	Used appropriately	Omitted	Used inappropriately
Periods	1087	482	123
Commas	73	230	8
Quotation marks	47	249	17
Question marks	34	30	3
All marks: First year	438	500	69
All marks: Second year	803	49	182

We can see from the table that some punctuation marks were easier for these children to use appropriately than others. Periods, which constituted the majority of punctuation marks, were supplied when necessary about two-thirds of the time, while question marks were supplied when needed only about half of the time. Commas and, especially, quotation marks were appreciably more difficult and usually omitted. (As a comparison figure, the children spelled 86% of the words in these texts appropriately. Similarly, words were capitalised when they should have been 86% of the time.) Periods made up about 87% of all punctuation marks the children used. The children as a whole were using punctuation quite a bit more proficiently in the second year of the study than in the first; they supplied obligatory punctuation 46% of the time in the first year and 62% in the second.

This summary of how these six children used punctuation is an overview that masks the great variability between them, which is what I will devote the rest of this chapter to discussing. Each individual child's profile is different from the overall profile in ways that reflect not only quantitative differences in how well they punctuated but qualitative differences in what their particular strengths and weaknesses were. Table 4.2 summarises the differences in their overall proficiency.

I will begin by discussing the least proficient user of punctuation, Elaine, and continue in order.

Table 4.2 Six children's use of punctuation

	Used appropriately	Omitted	Used inappropriately
Elaine	122	242	76
Rachel	153	188	12
Gordon	146	174	10
Vincent	138	151	9
Anna	284	171	15
Dana	411	75	29

Elaine

Except for a single extraneous comma in third grade, Elaine never used a punctuation mark other than a period, although there were occasions when she should have used commas, quotation marks, and question marks. Table 4.3 shows that periods were more likely than not to be omitted in her writing, and that she also included extraneous ones.

The following partial text is an example of how Elaine's stories were

Table 4.3 Elaine's use of periods

	Used appropriately	Omitted	Used appropriately
First year	37	99	41
Second year	85	57	34
Overall	122	156	75

frequently punctuated. (Spelling has been conventionalised but line divisions are as in the original.)

> One day I went to a christmas
> party we Had to. bring some.
> gifts. to the party I took
> cakes we drank some punch. it was
> time to open the gifts. I got
> some gum and a doll it was
> time for me to go home then my.
> mom came home...

Periods were not included in six obligatory spots in the text (including the final sentence). Of the six periods used, only two were appropriate. Of the other four, two were at the ends of lines, one before a prepositional phrase, and one (after 'to') idiosyncratic. Although Elaine's use of periods seems bizarre (many of her extraneous ones were unusually placed), they were not random but reflected incomplete understanding and internalisation of a variety of knowledge about punctuation, including rules for its use. For instance, on various occasions she stated that she used periods when there was a capital letter, at the end of a story or a section of it, or at the ends of sentences. Another time she said that periods are needed to break a story up and that it matters where they are placed but that she wasn't sure where to put them.

This state of affairs did not remain static, however. About a month after Elaine wrote the above story, she came to understand how sentence boundary punctuation works. There was a dramatic change in her use of periods, with omissions from then on occurring only rarely and extraneous periods occurring at reasonable syntactic boundaries such as between clauses or in place of question marks. A typical example read as follows (with spelling conventionalised):

> One day the sun came up. Me and Monica were going to town. Then

the sun was up. And it was brighting in our eyes. Then we couldn't see and we almost went off the road. Then we started to cry. But we crashed. Then the police came. And the ambulance. And we got in the hospital so that's how it all happened.

Although Table 4.3 shows appreciable growth from the first to the second year of the study, it understates the dramatic nature of the change. Table 4.4 divides Elaine's use of periods into those before and after her new understanding.

This is a clear-cut example of saltatory growth as described by Werner (1978): a qualitative change involving a sudden replacement of a lower-level process by a higher-level one. The explanation for this sudden change is very simple: the teacher had sat down with Elaine one day and helped her get a feel for the natural pauses in a text that indicate sentence boundaries, thus making the half-baked and dimly understood rules that she had been using no longer necessary.

Table 4.4 Discontinuity in Elaine's use of periods

	Used appropriately	Omitted	Used inappropriately
Before 1/83	60	159	64
1/83 and after	62	6	11
Overall	122	156	75

Rachel

Rachel used a variety of punctuation marks; she used periods appropriately about half of the time (omitting them the rest of the time) and was the most prolific user of question marks and exclamation points of the six children (using them 20 and 5 times respectively). Her major difficulty other than the omission of periods was failure to use quotation marks and the obligatory comma that precedes them (with the exception of the last piece she wrote in fourth grade, where one quotation was punctuated appropriately). That year she used far more quotations in her writing than she had the year before (25 as opposed to 2), but did not yet know how to punctuate them. Her use of periods, which accounted for the majority of her punctuation, showed substantial improvement from the first to the second year: the proportion of times she used a period when one was needed went from 42.4% to 61.3% of the total. Although general growth as a writer led her to omit more punctuation marks of one type (i.e. she had found uses for quotations in her writing but did not yet fully control their form), her use of punctuation in general was improving.

Gordon

Gordon's use of obligatory punctuation was confined almost entirely to periods and, in the latter part of fourth grade, quotation marks. He showed definite improvement in both; in third grade he omitted about half of all periods but in fourth grade less than a third. Once he discovered quotation marks, he used them appropriately most of the time; the occasions when he didn't were most likely due to forgetfulness. The rule he used for determining the placement of quotation marks was to place the first one after 'said' and the second one at the end of the quotation; this was usually appropriate, but resulted in his mistakenly punctuating an indirect quotation twice and mispunctuating a divided quotation once, producing the following result:

Intended: 'Little Knife,' said his father, 'Don't worry...'
Actual: Little Knife said 'his father don't worry...'

The result is an error something like that made by some of the children reading punctuation who were studied by Perera (see this volume). Gordon rarely used other punctuation marks, using commas only twice and omitting 50 of them, primarily (54%) those required before quotations. His one unusual punctuation mark was the one described at the beginning of this chapter, where he wrote a date with a reversed and normal comma enclosing the numerals, perhaps with the intent of setting it off in a way analogous to quotation marks. Gordon also used hyphens (which are editing marks rather than standard punctuation), hypothesising consciously that they are used when one comes to the end of a line and has letters left in the word, yet in practice often appropriately dividing words at syllable breaks. He also once invented a punctuation device; as he was writing the word 'football,' he decided its two parts should have a space between them, but smaller than usual because 'they go together.' This could perhaps be described as a half-space, serving as a written language morpheme to indicate compounds. (A week later, he wrote 'cupcake' with a hyphen, which he described as another way of showing that two words go together. This is, of course, a legitimate way of indicating some compounds in English.)

Vincent

Vincent showed the most dramatic improvement in punctuation of any of the six children between third and fourth grade, going from 29.0% to

65.9% appropriate use, a proportionate change of 124%. This was due primarily to a gradual improvement in his use of periods, which were virtually the only punctuation marks he ever used. Unlike Elaine, who showed a dramatic change in her use of periods, Vincent changed gradually from omitting most periods to omitting only a few, particularly in fourth grade. He also included a few extraneous periods, primarily between clauses. His only other problem with punctuation was the omission of almost all quotation marks, question marks, and commas, in both third and fourth grades. Vincent's attention to punctuation was clearly primarily limited to the use of periods; presumably in the future, as the use of periods became more automatic, he would have more attention available to devote to other types of punctuation.

Anna

Anna used periods appropriately about 85% of the time over the two-year period, with occasional omissions and even rarer insertions. Her use of periods changed only slightly from third to fourth grade; she basically understood their use, with occasional lapses. She used other punctuation marks occasionally, and was more likely to include them in fourth grade than in third. In fourth grade she occasionally used quotation marks in idiosyncratic ways:

She is saying rain", "rain go away…
My mother said "I "hope it snows…

Her overall use of punctuation was appropriate only 50% of the time in third grade and 75% in fourth and this was, to some extent, because of her use of a large number of virtually unpunctuated quotations in the first year.

Dana

Dana's use of punctuation was by far the most proficient of all the children, in both third and fourth grades. His use of periods was almost entirely appropriate by fourth grade (about 95% of the time, perhaps better than many adults). He was as likely to insert extraneous periods as to omit obligatory ones, although this involved only a few cases occurring primarily at clause boundaries. He was by far the most successful user of the more difficult comma and quotation marks, which he used appropriately 60.9% and 50.0% of the time respectively, as opposed to 24.1% and 15.9% for the children as a whole. Although Dana had a good understanding of punctuation in third grade, he was able to further refine it in fourth, showing increased control of every type of punctuation mark.

What Do These Six Children Tell Us?

First of all, as we examine the writing of these six children both as a group and as individuals, there is some evidence that they first focused their efforts on periods, and at some point began to pay increasing attention to other punctuation as well, with quotation marks emerging last. (Calkins, 1980, discovered that a group of third-grade children in a classroom where writing was a strong focus were aware of and used many different punctuation and editor's marks, suggesting that the limited number of symbols used by these six children is more likely to be due to limited experience within the classroom rather than any intellectual limitations of this age group.)

Elaine and Vincent were at a stage in their development where they usually used only periods. Gordon, Anna and Rachel used both periods and other punctuation, but were far less proficient in their use of the latter. It was only Dana, who had virtually mastered periods, who used quotation marks conventionally as much as half of the time.

Also, the children's use of punctuation improved dramatically from third to fourth grade. This occurred in the face of little if any instruction other than regular opportunity to read and write. These data certain imply that teachers do not have to be concerned that children will regress if not given formal instruction in punctuation; given regular opportunities to write, these children all moved toward greater proficiency. Cordeiro *et al.* (1983) described how difficult it is to teach explicit rules for punctuation, particularly periods; perhaps knowledge about punctuation can most readily develop through encouraging children to use punctuation in their writing and giving them feedback on an individual basis. However, there is certainly room in the writing curriculum for more focused instruction about punctuation, if it is of the kind that encourages children to think actively about the role of punctuation in expressing meaning and signalling sentence structure rather than simply learning sets of rules. (The conventions that are most readily expressed as workable rules, such as those for using commas in a series or with dates, are not usually very difficult for writers anyway, even young ones; conventions like the ones governing when to use commas to separate off clauses are harder to define and difficult for many adults to understand and use appropriately.)

Let me conclude with instructional suggestions for each of the six children I've described here. I offer some thoughts about mini-lessons or activities that respect their present state of development and would provide the little extra scaffolding needed to push them on to a more highly articulated understanding of this aspect of the written language system. (For further teaching ideas, see Wilde, 1992, particularly Chapter 7.)

For Elaine, who had finally reached a workable understanding of how and where to divide sentences, it would be interesting to invite her (and, as in all these examples, probably also a small group of other children with a similar level of understanding) to write in a brief learning-log format an answer to the question, 'How do you know where the periods go when you're writing a story?' Students could then share and discuss what they'd written and perhaps decide how they would want to share this knowledge with a younger, less proficient user of punctuation.

Rachel, who had only just discovered how to punctuate quotations, could be invited, along with others, to look at how a variety of text formats indicate to the reader who is speaking and when the speaker changes. In addition to the standard use of dialogue carriers that children have encountered in early reading since the days of 'Dick said, "See Spot run,"' they are also likely to be familiar with texts where a conversation is carried on without the speaker's being indicated at every turn, as well as books like *The Day Jimmy's Boa Ate the Wash* (Noble, 1984) and its sequels, where the entire text is dialogue. Play scripts, of course, use a different convention to indicate who is speaking; could these young readers convert a script to a story or vice versa (assuming, of course, an authentic purpose for doing so)? One should also not forget that children may be very familiar with the comic book conventions of using speech bubbles to surround speech.

Gordon, who took an active interest in punctuation marks like the hyphen and his own invention the half-space, could be encouraged to see how many different punctuation marks he could find and to determine if he could figure out how they are used. Many dictionaries have both punctuation guides or tables and illustrations of proofreader's marks that would be useful resources here. Vincent, whose use of punctuation marks was virtually limited to the period, would perhaps be another candidate for this activity; the heterogeneous grouping would allow a student like Gordon to explore the further reaches of the punctuational universe while also expanding the more limited perspective of one like Vincent.

Anna and Dana, the most successful users of punctuation among the six children, would perhaps have the least need for instruction, Anna because she was already developing rapidly as a user of punctuation and Dana because he was already so close to adult proficiency. Since any further issues in punctuation for them are likely to be idiosyncratic, they would perhaps be best served by a teacher who stayed tuned in to their ongoing use of punctuation in order to spot opportunities for teachable moments.

Dana, in particular, however, might enjoy sharing some of his expertise, either as a general punctuation consultant for the class as a whole or perhaps by writing a punctuation handbook for his peers.

For older and more proficient users of punctuation at whatever age, increased growth is likely to come through reading of increasingly more sophisticated materials, the writing of text structures of an increasing range of complexity, and, ideally, both the desire and the confidence to think consciously about how punctuation works, perhaps with the support of a teacher or peers. I have often thought it would be fun to organise a brief series of mini-lessons on the semicolon for university students; this versatile and relatively sophisticated symbol is used far too seldom by non-professional writers. Although I might draw on a rule or two, my major focus would be on finding good examples of semicolon use in published prose and encouraging students to describe its use in their own words and then apply it. What could be simpler? Who needs workbooks?

5 Conversations With Teachers About Punctuation

ANNE ROBINSON

Background

In recent years the British education system has been undergoing a large number of structural and curriculum changes. The British Government developed the notion of a National Curriculum. This was to be followed by all children at school and would be accompanied by national assessment at specific ages. Government-chosen committees decided, after various levels of consultation, what was to be taught in the curriculum areas. Prior to the existence of the National Curriculum, British schools were pretty free to teach what they wanted in the ways they wanted. Now, schools have to address the areas indicated in the National Curriculum and although in theory they are still free to choose how they teach these areas, the national assessments have had considerable impact upon what is taught, when it is taught and how it is taught. The National Curriculum began in 1991 with what is known as Key Stage 1. This covers the years from five to seven; what previously in British schools would have been called the infant school years. (It is vital to note that, for the purposes of this chapter, all references to the National Curriculum are to the DES (1989) documentation in use at the time of the teacher interviews.)

The Statement of Attainment for Level 2 for writing (representing what the most seven-year-olds would be expected to achieve) said the children should:

'Produce, independently, pieces of writing using complete sentences, some of them demarcated with capital letters and full stops or question marks.'

For Level 3, (which above average seven-year-olds would be expected to achieve), they should:

> 'Produce, independently, pieces of writing using complete sentences, mainly demarcated with capital letters and full stops or question marks.'

It is fair to say that in general, until the existence of the National Curriculum punctuation was not widely taught in the early years of British schooling. There was no expectation that by the age of seven children would have mastered many punctuation skills. It was something that was more usually left until the junior school (ages 7–11). As a consequence, it came as something of a shock to many teachers when the National Curriculum for English introduced very specific demands about what seven-year-old children should know about, and be able to do with, punctuation.

Children in Year 2 classes (six- to seven-year-olds) were assessed nationally for the first time in England in 1991. To assess their writing, children were asked to write a story and part of the assessment related to punctuation. Punctuation was not assessed independently of other areas in writing; children had to achieve the same level in all the components of writing. A failure on any one component prevented the child from achieving Level 2. And this is where the problem started! Soon after the first national assessment Head Teachers (Principals) were reporting that many children were writing at length very interesting stories, getting a reasonable level of handwriting and spelling but were being marked down as a whole because of poor achievement with punctuation. What had happened was that punctuation had become the criterial factor in determining a child's position on the writing assessment.

As this became clear, teachers expressed private concerns. There was a general feeling about it not being fair because the final judgment did not represent the overall ability of the children. Informal conversations with teachers, and particularly those working with children who were developing a high degree of confidence in their own writing ability, indicated disappointment and concern. It is important to recognise that this concern was being expressed by experienced teachers and head teachers. On the one hand, we had teachers who felt satisfied with the writing their children were doing (in some cases saying these children were 'good for their age'). On the other hand, we had the National Curriculum assessment indicating that these very same children did not make the level expected of average seven-year-olds.

Partly in response to these teachers concerns about punctuation, The

Punctuation Project was set up at the Manchester Metropolitan University. One of the first areas we decided to explore was teachers' own thinking and concerns about punctuation, as very little seemed to be known about this. As National Curriculum assessment of writing has continued, the requirements have been made more precise. At the time of writing it is clear that the new curriculum documents have become even more demanding. Teachers concerns are likely to increase as a result and more of their children may seem to be disadvantaged. In these circumstances it is, therefore, particularly important to consider the demands being made and to take seriously the unease which some teachers feel.

Rather than conduct formal interviews or use questionnaires, it was decided to approach the study in a more informal way in the initial stages. Informal interviews were carried out with a range of teachers of younger children. These conversations had an agenda but it was loose and both interviewer and interviewee would be free to talk about related areas of interest. It was also important that the teachers should understand that this was a genuine exploration of ideas and points of view and that no-one was seeking 'correct' answers or expecting them to represent anything other than their own interests and concerns.

The conversations focused on three interrelated areas: the teachers' own use and understanding of punctuation, their response to the National Curriculum demands, and their views about the teaching and learning of punctuation.

Where Are the Teachers Coming From?

Each conversation started with a question about the teacher's confidence when using punctuation in their own writing. One important aspect of teaching is feeling comfortable with the subject being taught. As all the teachers were well educated, literate and experienced writers, punctuation was not expected to be a problem for them. This assumption seemed to be borne out in the teachers' responses. Most of them responded positively, with some minor reservations, to the question, 'How do you feel about using punctuation in your own writing?'

'I feel very confident about it. I don't think it's quite as simple as some people think but I don't find it a problem.'

'At my own level, I would say very confident.'

'I think I feel OK most of the time.'

Those teachers who initially had reservations in their response to this question, indicated later that their problems were with a particular, more complex punctuation mark. For instance:

'Sometimes semi-colons. I never quite know whether to use a semi-colon or a colon.'

When asked what they did when faced with this decision, one replied:

'Probably leave it out. If in doubt leave it out. That's the slogan, isn't it?'

Another said:

'If I'm not overly confident I'll change what I'm saying so that I don't need that particular rule.'

However, in general they felt confident about their overall ability to punctuate text, especially as several of them indicated that they mainly wrote personal letters and there was a degree of flexibility in such writing.

The teachers' remarks were often accompanied by comments which revealed a clear perspective on the social status of punctuation. Some indicated that while confident with personal writing, they would always check more carefully if the letters were official ones, or the writing had a wider audience:

'Obviously, if it's an official letter I'm trying to be impressive, really. Trying to make it look as if I'm intelligent. If it's a letter to a solicitor or something or you know — you try to match up your image to what you think they might expect from the kind of person it's from.'

There was a clear concern that other people would make judgments about their level of literacy, or even of their intelligence, on the basis of their punctuation. Interestingly enough a couple of teachers suggested that this was one of the reasons for learning and using punctuation:

'I mean, part of it would be because you'd want them to think, "Oh, this person knows how to write".'

'I think one reason is to show someone else who might be reading my work that I understand the rules of grammar.'

They also noticed the absence of correct punctuation in the writing of other adults:

'If it's not there I notice it. You know, for example, letters that come from parents... In very rare cases you may have to go back and re-read because it wasn't quite clear, but I think what it does cause you to do is make a judgment, a judgment of the writer if it's not there... I think what you might be saying would not be very flattering, and it would be something that you would never, you know, you would never let that person know you thought it but it would be there at the back of your mind.'

Given that teachers, on the whole, feel confident about their ability to punctuate, how and where did they learn to do it? It seems that it cannot be assumed that their education will have included specific teaching about punctuation. For instance, when asked whether they could remember being taught about punctuation, several responded with comments like:

'Yes, I mean I wasn't really taught, well not really taught punctuation. Someone must have mentioned it to me in my life, but I'm from an era when it was "Oh, never mind your spelling or your punctuation, get your ideas down".'

On the whole, most could remember punctuation being there somewhere in their schooling, but being specific was more problematic:

'Very vaguely at school, yes, it was like sentences, capital letters and full stops...we didn't do grammar lessons as such or anything like that.'

'I can remember doing a lot of exercises where you had to put your speech marks in... It started in primary school I think. I think it did. But certainly, I mean I was brought up being taught English through a grammatical approach.'

'Not until Upper Juniors, and I can remember exercises where you had to put the capital letters and full stops. And then I can remember at secondary school some work on apostrophes. But I can't remember any more.'

Recalled experience of punctuation teaching indicated two main types of experience. On the one hand, there were what they called traditional 'complete the unpunctuated passage' exercises. These were usually re-called as happening in the later years of primary school (around 9–11 years). On the other, there was what they termed 'grammar', which they recalled happening in their secondary education (age 11 and onwards). Grammar was assumed to involve punctuation; in the 'doing' of grammar, one learned to punctuate. Parsing of sentences was mentioned, and there was talk of having 'little blue grammar books' in which sentences were taken apart and marked with different coloured lines. Only some of the teachers had this experience, and they indicated clearly that the recollection was not a favourable one. It could be that it contrasted too markedly with their notion of learning as revealed later in the conversations.

There are two problems with interpreting comments like the above. Children, when learning, may not be aware of 'teaching'; after all a lot depends upon how one defines the word 'teaching'. Carefully organised incidental learning situations may not be experienced by children as learning a particular topic. The second point is that remembering back to what happened in school is always difficult. However, whether these teachers were effectively taught or not, only a minority claim to be influenced by that teaching to any great degree.

We can be more certain in respect of what they remember about their teacher education. Given that teachers are expected to teach children to punctuate, one might anticipate that somewhere in their teacher education punctuation would have featured. However, with the exception of one person, none could remember the teaching of punctuation featuring anywhere during their teacher education. The one person who could, recalled only one short lecture. They all claimed that their teacher education courses did not help them to prepare for teaching punctuation. Given that the teachers completed their training across a wide span of time (the range was from 4 years ago to 25 years ago), it is clear that nothing much has changed where punctuation is concerned. More disturbingly, in view of widespread teacher concern about punctuation, is the fact that not one of the teachers had ever been on any in-service courses about writing which featured the teaching of punctuation.

Despite the absence of help in teaching punctuation, all the teachers felt confident about teaching it to young children. This may have something to do with how they perceive the level of demand. When asked how confident they felt about teaching young children to punctuate, they responded positively:

'Yes I do feel confident because I'm not doing it in a sort of formal way. It's just when I look at their writing and talk about what they've put down.'

This confidence was in their ability to handle punctuation as they believed it ought to be taught. However, these questions were in the initial part of the conversation before other more complex issues were raised. As will become clear later, this initial confidence was not as strong as they thought.

Reactions to National Curriculum Demands

The precise requirements were only made clear when the first assessment tasks were published. Evidence of attainment at Level 2 demanded that the child:

'Writes independently; separate "ideas" or sentences can be identified; at least two of these sentences begin with a capital letter and end with a full stop.'

Evidence at Level 3:

> 'Writes independently; ideas expressed in recognisable sentences; more than half the sentences correctly punctuated; in a long piece, any passage of more than 10 sentences may be assessed for punctuation.'

For people without experience of the development of young children's writing, asking a seven-year-old for only two sentences in a piece of writing to be correctly demarcated may not seem too onerous. Yet, teachers repeatedly said they were concerned about these demands. When asked about how they felt about the National Curriculum requirements some teachers had strong and direct views:

> 'Inappropriate.'

But why?

> 'It's inappropriate because I think for the children...a lot of them have the ability to write in terms of content...style...they have the ability to be fairly accurate with spelling, and consistent, and it seems to me that they are being penalised for things like full stops and capital letters because they haven't reached a point of understanding that I think comes with reading age.'

> 'I don't think they actually have a lot of experience of reading and writing to actually see the point to punctuation.'

> 'They are just on the edge of development in their writing and to teach them punctuation would stop that for some children...put them off, you know. I think they expect too much.'

> 'They are still becoming independent writers. I've got children who are brilliant writers, they've got great imaginations, so they want to get it all down. They won't actually put punctuation in. If you said to them remember the spelling, remember the punctuation, think about the story and all that, I don't think you'd get the quality.'

> 'I'm quite happy developing awareness in the children but that's not the same thing as having them do it. I think once awareness has been raised...and as the child's ability to write develops so they will develop the ability to punctuate...but to get them to do it at an early age I think it's a bit dodgy.'

In criticising the National Curriculum expectations, the teachers were not dismissing punctuation as unimportant either in the long term or the short term. In fact, as the following quotes indicate, they saw it as an important part of the young child's experience:

> 'When they're doing their own writing and beginning to use key words

in the writing, common spellings and things and have developed the content, I think it's time to start punctuation. I think it's important too, I don't think you should not teach it at all.'

'I think the National Curriculum is actually making me think more about punctuation. And again, because ultimately it's important...perhaps what I should be saying is that it's the stage that we're asking them to do it at that's wrong.'

'I think for Key Stage 2 it's a reasonable request. But I think for a seven-year-old, it's too much to ask for children who are only emergent writers really.'

The main area of concern seem to be the relationship between encouraging children to write with fluency and comfort, and the demand for inserting accurate punctuation. They clearly felt these to be contradictory expectations and were very explicit about not wanting to discourage children from enjoying writing by forcing them to pay attention to features they did not fully understand. They felt that the inherent difficulties of punctuating might result in children being forced to cope with concepts before they were ready. This was a constantly repeated worry:

'I think they are having to learn it before they are ready to understand it. Like when we had to learn our times tables before we had the mathematical aptitude for them.'

'I think teachers have stopped being able to look at a child's writing, seeing where the child is at, and then decide the next steps. It's almost as if the next steps are decided for you because of some outside influence.'

There was also the problem that some teachers felt they were being forced to teach what was in the National Curriculum rather than what they thought the children needed:

'I know we don't like to think we are teaching to the test; there should be broad and balanced options open to the children, but the way I look at it is, why should the children in this school be disadvantaged because they haven't done it?'

In some ways this is not the fault of the National Curriculum; nowhere in the documentation does it imply that children should be taught things they are not ready to cope with. If a child is deemed to be at a particular level of attainment they should be helped to move to the next level. However, it seems that the problem arises from what is thought by teachers to be a reasonable requirement for an average seven-year-old.

The teachers were concerned that the consequences of setting the standards too high would be that either the children or the teachers were appearing to fail:

> 'Children could write four or five pages of wonderful story — everything else — spelling and the lot, beautiful, and they'd be reduced to Level 1 because of the punctuation.'

Statements in official documents carry with them a degree of authority which makes them difficult to challenge. Statements in such documents are assumed to have a factual basis and to be based on evidence. When teachers find themselves in a position where their own experience challenges that of outside agencies who set themselves up as authorities, then a great deal of tension is created. In the first instance, to even think about challenging such authorities one has to feel confident in one's own point of view. It was clear that while the teachers in this study were confident in some aspects relating to punctuation and confident that their judgments about the children were well-founded, their initial expressions of concern were very general. They were in a position of simply feeling that it is 'not fair' to expect six-and-a-half to seven-year-olds to have to punctuate in order to be seen as average writers for their age and that the demand would cause failure and put children off writing.

These comments should be seen in context. They reflected what might be called an unreflective, conventional position. The teachers had never been expected to give a high status to punctuation and at times when they had tried something relating to punctuation it had often not worked well. However, as some of the teachers conceded, they did not know whether such achievements were actually possible as they had never systematically developed policies towards punctuation either as individuals, or as members of a school teaching team. As Chapter 1 in this volume has made clear, it is not surprising as there was so little information available to help them. On the positive side, as one of the above quotations indicates, these demands were at least forcing them to think seriously about the role of punctuation in their teaching and in young children's writing.

Teaching Punctuation and Learning to Punctuate

Most of the teachers said that the main difficulty for children was in working out what a sentence was. Notions of full stops and capital letters make little sense without some concept of sentence; after all, for the most part, what they mark are the boundaries of sentences. Teachers were acutely aware that what often appeared to many people outside education to be the most basic and easiest thing of all, was actually one of the most complex:

'I mean I've always thought, you've got to define things like sentences. Too many teachers in the past have said, "Go and write me a sentence." Probably nobody has ever said to the child what a sentence is.'

'The concept of sentence is very difficult. I think actually...how do you define a sentence? I mean, I tell my children that a sentence is something that you write down, that tells you something, and I try to give them examples. I just give them a word and say, "Does that tell you something?" and they sort of look, and then I'll say, "This is 'a'," and leave it like that. And I'll say, "Does that tell us some thing? No." And then you give them a sentence. "Oh, yes, that tells us something." But they still can't get the idea of a sentence.'

'What is a sentence? What on earth is a sentence? So you put a full stop at the end of a sentence. If you don't know what a sentence is, how do you explain what a sentence is? And the best I can do is say where you stop and start again and that's not a very clear cut explanation as to when you do, you know, stop and start again because you might stop and start again because you've run out of breath rather than because you've come to the end of a sentence as such. And then again, what's the difference between a comma and a full stop, in that sense, if you don't have the concept of what a sentence is?'

'Define a sentence...it makes sense. A sentence makes sense, and you can say it in one breath. It starts with a capital letter and ends with a full stop. That's what I'd say to my children mostly, that it has to make sense. When you say it, does it make sense? And do you feel like pausing at the end before you start the next part.'

'I can't define at sentence at all — certainly not to a six-year-old.'

'Well, a sentence to me is a complete thought really...completely one...or you've come to the end of that, you're going to start something different now, so you put a capital. I don't know how I teach it really, its just — caught not taught, I think.'

Even a quick glance at the above quotations reveals that there are some major problems. Those explanations, given to another adult, are somewhat unclear, so how would they appear to a young child? While it would be easy to criticise the teachers, their problems are real ones to which there are not simple answers. (See Chapter 1 and Arthur's chapter in this volume.) It is easy to find very different definitions of sentences in handbooks on punctuation, and none of those definitions are ever complete and would certainly not be comprehensible to young children. It is unfortunately the case that we do not always take a breath after a sentence (try hearing such pauses when the news is being read on a radio programme), and what does it mean to say a sentence makes complete sense? As much complete sense as a paragraph, a page, a chapter? And who is to say that a word cannot make complete sense in many circumstances? The predicament expressed by the teachers does not represent a failure on their part; it is a reflection of the unrecognised complexity of giving explanations about punctuation to young children.

So how do they set about guiding the children to gain a sense of what a sentence is? Most seems to rely on understanding the role of intonation and pauses which accompany reading. Reading was mentioned by most of the teachers as being very important to developing understanding of punctuation. This was partly to come from the experience of reading aloud from books and partly from being asked to read aloud, or listen to someone else reading aloud, their own work:

> 'It's very much a natural progression that comes with reading especially.'

The majority of teachers talked about reading without pauses as a way of getting children to understand where full stops go. Intonation and pauses are seen as more useful than grammatical explanations, although the relationship between intonation and pauses is sometimes rather unclear:

> 'I would tend to stress intonation rather than grammatical things. They can actually hear the intonation, to take a breath, or the intonation in your voice and they get a lot of clues from that.'

> 'In their reading, like when they are not stopping at full stops, I'd tell them to breathe there.'

> 'I think I'd use the old — read a passage without it and say, you know "Look what's happened to me. Why, why can't I breathe?" And that actually does work. I wouldn't use their own writing either; I would use a passage from a book or something I had written. Because it denigrates what the child has written to make it sound silly, and to have any effect and to get the child to realise what you are trying to get at, you've got to look red in the face and out of breath.'

> 'If I've got a little group and they are actually writing something and they're having a quick look through what they've done, I will read it out, and I will read it as they've written it and I'll say, "I'm going blue in the face, look, where am I going to stop?" You know try and make it amusing so that you know, it does put it over to them. I'll say, "There's no comma or anything there. I don't know where to stop, take a breath or do anything. You're going to have me blue in the face."'

> 'As they get older, well not necessarily, as they become more fluent

readers, we do begin to talk about aids that are there to help you read with some expression, and if you wanted to read this book for your friend. So a lot of children, because they are fluent readers, we'll talk about changing your voice after you've seen a full stop.'

'I think if the children were fluent in reading and that they knew where to pause and could scan along to the end of a sentence and they knew where to take a breath. Whereas some others would just take a breath anywhere, even if it's not the end of a sentence.'

Very few teachers mentioned the fact that the child's own reading may not provide a good model to refer to in the early stages. On the other hand, they often talk about 'fluency' in reading being a sign that children might be ready to begin discussing punctuation. With this we enter into a circular argument; if a child is already fluent then they are already using intonation which takes them beyond the halting word-by-word reading so common in beginning readers. In this case, quite often their reading may come close to the structure shown by punctuation. Few would argue that this would seem to be a sensible time to talk about things with the children. If we study the National Curriculum documentation, however, we find that reading with intonation is a Level 3 requirement and so only the most able children in Key Stage 1 are expected to have reached that level of attainment. Therefore, to expect 'average' children to use this as the basis for their own punctuation seems somewhat strange. It is a case of mismatched requirements again:

'I think if the children were fluent in reading and that they knew where to pause and could scan along to the end of a sentence and they knew where to take a breath. Whereas some others would just take a breath anywhere, even if it's not the end of a sentence.

Would the way a child reads out loud influence it, do you think?

Well that's the way we try and do it. For instance some big books have speech marks and I might do a class activity and I would encourage children to put intonation into their voices… I've tried it with full stops as well, but it's actually a bit difficult with children to be able to feel them.'

In spite of the fact that many of the teachers mentioned meaning as their reason for using punctuation in their own writing, and that they had been taught it grammatically in secondary school, only one or two mentioned these as ways of approaching the development of understanding in the children. This may not be surprising as grammatical knowledge is neither expected by the National Curriculum until upper junior or lower secondary level, nor seen as part of a teacher's own agenda for children of this age.

However, for teachers who recognised the problems with describing punctuation as replacing intonation and pauses, and for some who seemed particularly aware of grammatical influences, an attempt to introduce some aspects of grammar could not be ignored:

> 'We'll talk about spacing and we'll talk about an idea, and then we'll talk about verbs, doing words, and nouns and collecting all these together to make them all go together, and you've got to have them all set in a particular order to make... I mean it's a long process but I do see it being learned.'

> 'I think, to me, ...constructing a sentence and using a verb and a noun is something that goes alongside using a comma, and a full stop, to me. I think it's difficult to separate them but I understand that it's difficult. So yes, the grammatical side of it has got to be part of it.'

This teacher, while making a claim about grammatical knowledge, had earlier spoken about using mainly intonation to help the children. When asked about this she answered:

> 'A lot of things I do for myself I don't do for them...it would be just too confusing. If I define it in a way it should be defined, they wouldn't know what I was talking about. I would hope by the stage that you wanted them to do it they would be pretty good readers, they would have had a great exposure to print. I think the more you're exposed to things, the more you're internalising what you've seen. So then I think you could begin to talk to them about what is a sentence. But I really think I'd be at the top end of Key Stage 2 or secondary level, because I'd want to then start talking about where verbs fit into this definition.'

The teachers in the group had very varied opinions about the relative difficulty of punctuation marks. In terms of order of difficulty, the National Curriculum mentions capital letters, full stops and question marks being learnt and used first. Later, children are expected to learn and use exclamation marks and inverted commas for direct speech. Commas are not expected to be used until the age of eleven and then only by the highest achieving children. Colons and semi-colons are not mentioned specifically in the Programmes of Study or the attainment targets.

When first asked the question 'Forgetting the National Curriculum demands, do you think there is an order in which punctuation marks should be introduced?', the response was invariably that full stops and capital letters were an obvious place to start. However, it was surprising how many hesitated and began to change their response as they realised that previous answers had indicated just how difficult these were for young children. It was almost as if it was an automatic response to say that full stops were easiest but when they actually thought about it, both common sense and their own experience with their children suggested this was not necessarily the case:

'Actually, the way you are talking to me, I'm beginning to realise that maybe there is...that what I thought was the order of doing things...that there are other things that might be easier that the children would understand and have greater success with.'

The sense of discovery was very explicit but it was not an isolated incident. It is difficult to capture a tone of voice or the look which convinces you that the person being questioned is reconsidering or reformulating an idea, but often in the interviews as the teachers began to talk about their experience of the children's work it was clear that their initial responses had become problematic.

Different marks varied greatly in the perceived level of difficulty and it is possible that it depends on whether one is considering the degree to which a child might be able to use the mark accurately or whether it can be explained easily. For example, speech marks were thought by several teachers to be within the grasp of the young children with whom they worked:

'It probably is. Yes, it probably is. In fact, it's strange, because the children who I've introduced that to were generally, in the main, successful, not only that time but in subsequent writing and the same goes, believe it or not, for things like exclamation marks...the children love just giving a word when somebody speaks and this exclamation mark.'

'Probably easier than full stops, because I tend to use a lot of speech bubbles, and again it's easier to demonstrate this is what someone is saying, and if you use speech bubbles quite a lot and the person is saying: "That's the bit that goes in there" it's then easier, again using a book, to point them out and say: "Look, instead of drawing a speech bubble in this book they're using these little signs called speech marks." And you can get the explanation over in that way.'

Not everyone shared this point of view:

'I know you get the odd child that you can talk to about quotation marks and things, you know, that somebody's just spoken...mainly though, it's not a deliberate teaching policy but it would not be an expectation.'

The question mark was an interesting punctuation mark to discuss. At one level it has a function quite different from a full stop yet is almost always is used to mark the end of a sentence. Thus its usage is inevitably tied up with the function of the full stop. For some teachers this made it more difficult:

> 'Well, a question mark again is probably in the same category as a full stop, but it has the added difficulty because children are not always able to distinguish the difference between what we would call a sentence and a question, and I think really question marks are probably one of the most difficult forms of punctuation, even though you talk about the key words of questions being "what", "who", "why", "where" and whatever, but sometimes when you read the printed word, there are questions and it's not got any of those words in. I've just had it with some children reading yesterday where there was one word and then a question mark.'

> 'And the question mark, I think that's quite hard. I think it's hard to understand what a question is when they are writing in their own writing.'

While other teachers felt that being associated with questions made them easier than full stops:

> 'I think they probably are…you know at the end of sentences, because I think when someone's asked a question there's a natural stop. I think they'd find it easier to find the right place, but full stops are hard.'

> 'I think they're just nice to do. I mean, I think it's an appealing shape. And the other thing, I think if you have the sort of interactive displays that people should have, then they are going to be there, aren't they?'

In a similar way, there were differences of view about the exclamation mark:

> 'Yes, well I find actually I've noticed some of them using exclamation marks and I think it's because I've used them. I've usually put a message on the computer for them.'

> 'Well I think they might enjoy using them. For instance, if you do a sort of firework way of putting them — a great big exclamation mark — because you want them all to go "Ooh!"'

> 'Not young children — not unless it's an absolute definite one.'

As far as the teaching and learning of punctuation are concerned, there are all kinds of things to consider. In an area where so much has been taken for granted there is still so much more to explore. The teachers were raising some very important question and just beginning to recognise some of the complexities.

Conclusions

The first thing that needs pointing out is that the conversations with these teachers were, for most of them, the first time anyone had talked to them about punctuation. Being present at the discussions and listening to the tapes afterwards convinced me, in a way impossible to capture in transcriptions, that many of the teachers were thinking explicitly and seriously about punctuation for the first time. In several cases initial unreflective answers were changed as the teachers thought issues through. Utterances like 'Well, I suppose, on thinking more about it...' showed that they were being confronted with issues which had not been raised with them previously. This is of course quite consistent with their responses which indicated no work about punctuation during their initial teacher education or since on any in-service course. A number of the questions made them really have to think about what they believed or what they did. It almost seemed at times as if the questions themselves were helping to formulate their ideas. So, one very obvious implication of this small study is that punctuation needs to be put on the agenda at all levels: initial teacher education; in-service courses; and in staff room discussions.

The second important thing to note is that talking about punctuation is not always easy. At times the teachers had some difficulty explaining their ideas clearly. Of course, unprepared talk often looks somewhat confused when transcribed and seeing what you say can be rather disconcerting. In some of the examples it is clear that the teachers were thinking and rethinking as they were talking. But above and beyond that, the teachers also found it quite difficult at times to put into words their thinking and their meanings. It is the case that some aspects of punctuation are difficult to explain concisely and if the teachers are having difficulty explaining to another adult it is even more likely that they will have difficulty explaining to a child. However, we can not overlook the fact that the teachers may not have been altogether sure in their own knowledge about punctuation. Knowing how to do something is not the same as being able to describe in detail, or explain what you are doing. There seems to be a case for not only opening up discussion at a general level but providing information about punctuation at a particular level.

It is also clear that the claims made by the teachers about the teaching and learning of punctuation were fairly vague, and generally involved bits and pieces that did not cohere into a clear set of strategies. Despite the claims that were made, progress was seen as being a product of general kinds of experiences. Teachers did not seem particularly clear about the nature of their own role or of that of the children. It is of course possible that was a problem of explication and that in practice the teachers were consistent and coherent in the ways they taught punctuation. This study could not address that issue. However, the honesty of the teachers, and their ready admissions about uncertainties, imply that this would not be so. It is not surprising that teachers should be less than coherent in their approaches. As Chapter 1 in this volume has indicated, there is relatively little to help teachers in this area. It goes without saying that there is a need for more research. Perhaps a simple starting point would be for teachers to examine what their children can do, what they find easy, what things work and begin to consult with other teachers in order to share their findings.

As far as external demands are concerned, none of the teachers felt confident that the demands of the National Curriculum could be met. This response could be seen as just part of a general disenchantment with the National Curriculum, or perhaps one could be justified in suggesting that teachers who are not well-trained in an aspect of the curriculum have a right to feel that they cannot meet such demands. While there may be some measure of truth in both these, it must be remembered that in this instance the claims of the teachers are no less valid than those of the National Curriculum requirements. As has been explained elsewhere in this book, systematic study of what might be expected at various levels of schooling just does not exist. The claims of the teachers are at least made on evidence of their own experience, which in the absence of any more rigorous research has to count as acceptable. At the very least, they have to be listened to seriously.[1]

Finally, what does all this imply for the teachers and the children? Having thought carefully about what the teachers said and the concerns they expressed, I am convinced that above all else the teachers have the children's learning foremost in their minds. Their major concerns centre around whether what is being demanded is reasonable. The problem seems to be that no-one knows. Yet again, we are forced to acknowledge that the prescriptivism of the National Curriculum does not rest upon actual evidence. It may be quite reasonable to expect this level of achievement. What is clear is that teachers are not at this moment convinced that it is. Until there is serious study of how children develop understanding of punctuation and what conditions are most efficacious, then the punctuation experiences of children in schools are likely to remain somewhat confusing.

Perhaps the most useful thing that can be said about the National Curriculum demands is that they have brought punctuation to the forefront of discussion. It is important to keep it there until we have a firmer foundation on which to base both teaching and assessment requirements.

Note

1. Since the above interviews were carried out and the chapter written, a new version of the English National Curriculum has appeared (DfE, 1995). Far from listening to what teachers have said about the difficulties involved, the new version makes life even more demanding. This version expects most children by the end of Key Stage 1 (typically seven-year-olds) to use capital letters, full stops, question marks and begin to use commas. By the end of Key Stage 2 (typically eleven-year-olds) they are to use exclamation marks, commas, inverted commas and apostrophes to mark possession. By the end of Key Stage 4 (a typical sixteen-year-old) they should be using the full range of punctuation marks.
    However, alongside these extra demands has been a scaling down of the assessment requirements. In the 1995 SATs, Key Stage 1 children were expected to meet only two out of the three criteria for each level; failings on one criteria, punctuation, would no longer reduce children's overall scores. Thus, teachers concerns have been addressed as far as assessment is concerned, but not as far as the underlying expectations are concerned.

6 Learning About Punctuation: A Look at One Lesson

CANDICE ARTHUR

Introduction

How punctuation can be taught to young children is a problem faced by all teachers of young children. The difficulty is currently compounded in Britain by the demands (at the time of writing) of the National Curriculum, which suggests that children by the age of seven should:

> understand the nature and characteristics of a sentence

and

> learn to write in sentences and to demarcate sentences with capital letters and full stops or question marks. (DfE, 1993)

Although punctuation is often cited as a 'basic skill' (in the British National Curriculum, for example), very little is known about how the skill is acquired. Teachers receive negligible help with teaching punctuation, be it from teacher training courses, training days, or books (see Robinson, this book). This is largely because it is not clear what is the best method for teaching punctuation, and little is understood about how it is learned. As Ivanic (1988) remarks, having pointed out ambiguities and difficulties with most teachers' approaches to teaching punctuation:

> I ought to have something to offer in their place. This is not so easy. The main finding of this study was in fact that there are no simple solutions. (p. 22)

However, some research has been undertaken which has bearing on methods of teaching punctuation. Calkins (1980) reports a study of two classes of third-grade children. One of the teachers believed in teaching punctuation in context — that is, allowing children to use punctuation for their own ends in their own writing, while the other teacher approached punctuation through the use of drills and exercises. After a year Calkins found that the children who had no formal instruction had learned punctuation 'more effectively' than those whose instruction consisted of exercises.

Cordeiro, Giacobbe & Cazden (1983) used folders of writing from a class of first-grade children taught by Giacobbe to analyse the progress made in learning to use three punctuation marks: apostrophes, quotation marks and full stops. The approach of this teacher appears to have been similar to the more successful method employed in the Calkins study above, and was based on conferences with individual children about their writing in progress. Skills, including punctuation, were not brought into focus until the final, or editing, stage of production, while the primary focus was always content. One of the authors' conclusions was that teachers who concentrate on skills at the expense of content may actually be doing their children a disservice when it comes to learning punctuation.

Despite being about learning in classrooms, the two studies cited above do not actually offer a picture of how such learning takes place within classrooms. Cordeiro, Giacobbe & Cazden (1983) stated:

> We realize that...children have many sources of information in addition to the teacher: notably, other children and a wide variety of written texts. We have no way retrospectively to track children's use of these sources of information about punctuation... (p. 325).

Indeed while there are many gaps in our knowledge of how children learn to punctuate, nothing at all has been written which locates the learning of punctuation firmly within the classroom context, and thus offers what Barton (1994) terms 'an ecological approach'. Punctuation is not learned in a vacuum; nor is it invented out of nothing. Children's data for developing knowledge of punctuation exists in many forms, but much of it can be found in classrooms. Children see punctuation in a range of printed material, they see teachers using punctuation in writing demon-strations, they hear teachers talk about punctuation, they may hear other children talking about punctuation and they may have their punctuation marked. They may receive explicit teaching in punctuation either directly from a teacher or through undertaking exercises on handouts or in books. The knowledge of punctuation that children develop results from a meeting of their minds with a variety of the above experiences.

In this chapter I examine one source of data for young children, the demonstration of writing by the teacher. My own research project began as an investigation into young children's concepts of punctuation. In the course of this quest I spent numerous hours as an observer in Year 1 (age

5–6) and Year 2 (age 6–7) classrooms. The reason for using such an approach to collecting data arose from the realisation that data collected out of context was significantly less valuable than the rich data which could be collected through being present before, during and after writing events. As a way of attempting to overcome this possible shortfall, I carried out intensive observation in two classes over a period of one year. This allowed me to witness a variety of writing lesson events. One such event forms the basis of this chapter, and I intend to analyse it in the context of teaching and learning punctuation. The event I am describing is relatively typical of a kind of instruction observable in many infant classrooms, and through the analysis I wish to highlight some of the difficulties inherent in teaching punctuation to young children.

The Event

The event took place in a Year 2 class of 30 six- and seven-year-old children, and consisted of a teacher writing her own 'news' for the children as a demonstration of the kind of writing she expected from them and was followed by the children writing their own 'news'. The 'demonstration' was a common practice used by this particular teacher for introducing a writing task. The children sat cross-legged on the carpet while the teacher stood at an easel with a large blank piece of paper attached to it. She wrote onto the paper with a felt pen, talking to the children as she did so. The texts are reproduced in Example 6.1 with the teacher's written words on the left and her spoken commentary on the right. Included are all comments concerning punctuation; remarks about spelling and handwriting — which were also made — are summarised at the end. The teacher did not ask the children for suggestions of ideas or vocabulary as she wrote.

There were some additional comments made about spelling and handwriting. They were to do with: writing a 'g' through the line rather than on top of the line; not confusing 'd's and 'b's; remembering 'finger spaces'; and spelling 'went' and 'the' correctly.

Having finished the writing, Mrs T. says, 'When we've finished writing in the top infants (an older British name for this age group) we read it back, because sometimes we can make silly mistakes that we don't mean to.' A child is chosen to come to the board and read the writing aloud. At the exclamation mark the child reads with no particular expression. Mrs T. says, 'How are you going to say that with the exclamation mark there?' The child reads it again, this time shouting the last word.

This episode took approximately 13 minutes. Afterwards the children were told to go to their desks and to write their own news in their writing

Example 6.1

Writing on the board	Talk of teacher and children
	"What must I begin with?"
	A child replies, "Capital letter."
On Friday I went...	"I must put a capital 'I'
	because I'm so important."
to a bonfire. It	
was a huge bonfire.	"I'll put a full stop here."
I saw the flames	
they were yellow and	
red they looked like	
they were dancing in the	
night sky.	"I've finished telling you about the bonfire now so I'll put a full stop."

At this point a child says: "Miss, you forgot to put a full stop after red." Mrs T: "Well, yes, I could put one there. Good girl — you could put one there." She writes it in, saying, "So what comes next?" A few children reply, "Capital letter." Mrs T. changes 'they' to 'They'. She carries on writing on the same line after 'night sky'.

| ...I heard a | |
| great big bang | Having written this, |

Mrs T. says, "Now, what could I put there instead of just a full stop?" Children reply: "Comma"; "Question mark". Mrs T. says: "No, it's a little bit difficult. You might have seen it. It's an exclamation mark." As she writes it in, one or two children mutter, "Oh, yes." Mrs T. explains,"Because it's .." She reads the sentence and the children join in, shouting the last word. Mrs T. says: "It's like a full stop."

...The	
bang was a silver firework	
in the sky.	"I've finished talking about the firework now, so I've put a full stop. Now I'm going to tell you what I was wearing, because it was a very cold night."

Example 6.1 (*cont.*)

...I had to wear my hat and my large coat.	"Now, who do you think might have come with me?" The Children reply, "Mr T."
...Mr T. came with me.	"Why have I put a capital letter for Mr T.?" The children reply: "Because it's a name."

books. After 22 minutes the children stopped writing and lined up to go into assembly.

Analysis

At first sight the very typicality of this event might almost make it seem a non-event. However, it is the commonness and hence the easy acceptance of such occurrences that makes them worth examining closely. For these children a significant proportion of their indirect instruction in writing was carried out in this kind of way, and it is possible that the common everyday practices in classrooms generally are those which are likely to have the most impact on children's learning.

A number of specific questions are raised by consideration of this episode.

(1) What is the purpose of the exercise?
(2) What is the nature of the explanations given?
(3) What explanations are not given?
(4) What knowledge does the teacher assume the children to have?
(5) What do the children appear to know about punctuation before the event and after the event.

What is the purpose of the exercise?

The main purpose of the exercise appears to be to serve as a series of reminders of the conventions of writing. The teacher's emphasis is on spelling and punctuation: there is no discussion directly about the ideas contained in the piece. The only 'new' piece of information seems to be the use of the exclamation mark, although the teacher is not sure at the outset whether the children already have this knowledge. It is interesting to consider whether the emphasis on conventions is typical practice in classrooms. It would seem that the teacher's approach in this instance corroborates the evidence of Bennett *et al.*, that most teachers emphasise the conventions of writing over the content. Could it be that while teachers intellectually consider ideas to be more important, in reality their immediate concerns lie with the 'basics' of spelling, punctuation and handwriting? As suggested above, this would be no surprise in light of the demands made of teachers to 'produce the goods'.

One cannot be sure how such an event appears from the point of view of the child. What kinds of messages are the children being given about writing and its purpose? On a different occasion one of the children in this class, after her teacher had suggested what they could write down about the growth of a bean, said to me: 'How does she expect us to write all that? We can't hardly spell yet.' Raban (1986), asking children what they thought writing was for, found some confusion, the majority of the children interviewed seeing it as 'for when you grow up' (p. 6). Michel (1994) who investigated the child's view of reading, bases her account around the perturbing comment made by one six-year-old: 'I used to think reading was making sense of a story, but now I know it is just letters.' This suggests how school experience can distort a child's view of learning, and how it is possible that teachers can unwittingly create an impression that, for instance, writing is spelling, or reading is 'just letters'. (Further examples of children's attitudes to writing can be found in a booklet produced by the National Writing Project (Nelson, 1990).)

What is the nature of the explanations given?

The teacher offers explanations for a number of specific items of punctuation. These are:

(a) capital letters;
(b) full stops;
(c) exclamation marks.

I will look at each of these in turn.

Capital letters

Capital letters are used in the piece for:

(i)   starting the writing ('What must I begin with?');
(ii) the personal pronoun 'I ('because I am so important');
(iii) a person's name ('Why have I put a capital for Mr T.?');
(iv) following a full stop ('So what comes next?'). Although this is equivalent to starting a new sentence, the teacher at no point refers to the concept of 'sentence'.

(i) *'What must I begin with?'*

The children's response to the question 'What must I begin with?' is

'Capital letter'. For the children in this class, this is the learned answer to a recognised question. After all, their response could have been: 'An interesting idea'; 'A good word'; or 'A sharp pencil'. Similarly ritualistic is the children's response to 'What comes after a full stop?' Their answer is in terms of the following letter being a capital; it does not in this instance refer to the concept of a new sentence. While the exchange demonstrates knowing the answer to a question, it does not necessarily demonstrate understanding of the principle; nor does it necessarily lead to application of the knowledge. Hence, although a large proportion of the children on this occasion responded with 'Capital letter', less than half the children subsequently used capital letters to begin their own writing, while even fewer used a capital letter to begin a second sentence. The latter is a more complex problem, requiring further discussion below, since it involves an understanding of the relationship between punctuation and the concept of sentence.

No explanation is offered for why a capital letter is required at the beginning. Indeed, it is difficult to think of an explanation — a child might consider that it is easy enough to see where the writing begins because there is nothing before it, so the use of a capital letter to indicate the beginning might seem superfluous. Similarly difficult to comprehend might be the need for a capital letter following a full stop — the full stop does the job of showing where the sentence ends, so is it really necessary to follow it with a capital letter as well? It is certainly the case that many children who show some understanding of the use of full stops neglect to follow them with a capital letter. Also required, of course, is the knowledge that capital letters are different from lower case letters, and the ability to reproduce and differentiate between lower and upper case forms of the same letter. Therefore, when children are able ritualistically to cite the rule 'A sentence begins with a capital letter and ends with a full stop' there is no guarantee that they have an understanding of what constitutes a capital letter, that they know the capital forms of each letter, that they have concept of a sentence, or know what is the real purpose of either a full stop or a capital letter.

(ii) *'Because I am so important.'*

The need to capitalise the personal pronoun 'I' again defies extensive explanation. Indeed, the German *'ich'* (from which the English form is derived) and French *'je'* do not take initial capitals. In English the accusative and dative form 'me' takes no capital either. The teacher here offers the reasoning that 'I am so important' — a frequent and apparently sensible explanation. However, it is conceivable that a child will not consider her/himself as important as the teacher. One child in this class wrote 'i' in his news one day. His neighbour told him, 'You need a capital — because it's you — you're important.' The boy looked at her, but did not change it. I said, 'You are important, Stefan, aren't you?' He smiled at me, and shook his head. Similarly, can it really be fair — particularly in the light of constant reminders that we should be caring and sharing — to give 'I' a capital but not 'you'? According to Partridge (1977), the historical explanation is as follows:

> The capital I was established by early printers, mainly to avoid the ambiguity that had been caused by a confusion of such variant forms as i, j, I; more precisely, the use of I (for ego) was a specialisation of writing a 'long' i when the letter stood alone. (p. 109)

Small wonder that teachers devise alternative explanations for young children.

It would seem that it is only through repetition of the 'capital I' rule that it is likely to be remembered. Nevertheless, from my own observation of children's writing it is far more common for children to remember to capitalise 'I' than for them to remember to capitalise the beginning of a sentence. For example, a child in this class predicting the outcome of an experiment with beans wrote in one section: 'I tinc it whil Not grow', and in the next section: 'it whil grow' (neither contained a full stop). It is possible that this is due to the 'I' rule being relatively simple — it is always a capital when it stands alone, while rules offered for sentences — as pursued below — are anything but simple.

(iii) *'Why have I put a capital letter for Mr T.?'*

The children's response, 'Because it's a name', again suggests a learned response to a question. Many children who subsequently included names in their writing did not capitalise them; others capitalised some names and not others in the same piece of writing. Although no further explanation was given on this occasion, two days previously the same teacher had said: 'You always use a capital letter for a name — because there's only one Michael Evans, only one Gemma Honners [names of children in the class], and each one of you is very important.' At this point a child raised her hand and said, 'Miss, there are four Samanthas.' Whilst causing some amusement (at least to the adults present) this response suggests the difficulty of finding simple explanations that cover all cases. I have also witnessed the children in this class debating whether 'bear' should be capitalised or not. Those in favour suggested it should have a capital letter because it was a name. Such examples highlight the fact that many instructional devices rely on assumptions about the children's understanding; in this case a rather specific concept of 'name' is required.

Pressey & Campbell (1933) investigated ninth-grade children's use of capitalisation and discovered that 'the errors in capitalization were in large part explainable, logical, and understandable; they were far from being random or senseless' (p. 197). For example, capitals were used for words the children considered to be important, or common nouns which were capitalised in the title continued to be capitalised in the body of a piece of writing (see Anderson, this book). If these children were writing German they would be correct to capitalise all nouns, which demonstrates the apparent arbitrariness of our grammatical rules. For young children they might seem very arbitrary indeed.

(iv) *'So what comes next?'*

The use of the full stop will be discussed below, but there is a clear suggestion here that full stops are followed by capital letters. The question 'So what comes next?' seems to assume that the children know the answer. Their response suggests that they do know the answer, but the evidence of their own writing implies otherwise. Possible reasons for this include: children do not connect answers to verbal questions with applying the answer to their own writing; children forget to apply their knowledge; children do not consider it an important aspect of their writing; or the children have learnt a response which they do not understand. The issue of ritualistic learning arises again, and begs the question of its effectiveness as an aid to children's learning.

Full stops

The teacher in this episode offers one of a number of explanations commonly given for the use of full stops. Such rules tend to rely on one of the strands of reasoning associated with full stops, namely sound, sense, subject or syntax. They include statements such as: 'Put a full stop when you need to take a breath', 'Put a full stop when your voice drops' and 'Put a full stop when it makes sense'. Sadly, however, these kinds of explanation often fail as methods for determining the use of a full stop. This is largely because the full stop cannot be used consistently correctly until an understanding of the concept of 'sentence' is achieved. As Ivanic (1988) states, 'learning to punctuate is inseparable from learning to write in sentences'. And, as Cordeiro, Giacobbe & Cazden (1983) point out, 'Unfortunately for the ease of instruction, a "sentence" is in the end a formal syntactic category, and explanations that rely on non-syntactic criteria inevitably produce errors' (p. 331). Given the absurdity of presenting six-year-olds with a rule such as 'Put a full stop after you have used a subject, a finite verb and a predicate' (which in itself can be problematic as a failsafe strategy), what can teachers do? It seems to me that there is no short-term adequate answer.

The teacher in the event under discussion uses a change in subject as a guideline for a new sentence. Unfortunately her own writing demonstrates the shortfall of this method, as she produces prose which is grammatically incorrect:

> I saw the flames they were yellow and red they looked like they were dancing in the night sky.

One of the children points out that there should be a full stop after 'red'. It is not clear how the child knows this, but she appears to be in no doubt. The teacher, although she accepts the child's suggestion, seems to treat the full stop in this position as optional — in grammatical terms, however, either a full stop or a semi-colon is not optional but compulsory. The writing as it stands also requires some kind of punctuation mark after 'flames' — a colon, a semi-colon, a dash, or a full stop. To explain this in simple terms of either sense or prosody would be almost impossible — an explanation is not attempted and the non-sentence stands.

My experience of presenting a wide range of people, including young children and educated adults, with an unpunctuated passage has demonstrated the frequency of this kind of error. Given the text:

> Jenny was a hen she lived on a farm,

almost all children and a high proportion of adults either omitted to insert any punctuation, or inserted a comma after 'hen'. In simple terms I can offer only the arguable explanation that, without changing any of the words — such as substituting 'who' for 'she', 'Jenny was a hen she lived on a farm' consists of two separate statements, each of which contains a subject, a verb and a predicate, and therefore require separation by some form of final punctuation. If, as I suggest, such errors in sentencing are common in adults, is it reasonable to expect young children to learn so easily to write in sentences? If it is considered reasonable and necessary, how can teaching it effectively be achieved? The British National Curriculum for 1993 (DfE, 1993) requires children at the age of seven to be able to write in sentences, but offers teachers almost no help with fulfilling the requirement.

Exclamation marks

The exclamation mark is described in terms of it being 'like a full stop', but having a different sound — the teacher demonstrates by reading the word 'bang' loudly. Again the problem with such an explanation is that it covers only one aspect of the way in which punctuation is used, but it is difficult to conceive of any other simple but foolproof method of explaining the use of an exclamation mark. The children's writing produced after this event included exclamation marks only when the word 'bang' was used, for example: 'The fierwoke went bang! and pot.' This is an understandable and perhaps inevitable outcome.

What explanations are not given?

Consideration of what comments or explanations were not given suggests certain implicit choices made by the teacher. These choices might have been made for a number of reasons: (a) the teacher assumed the children to understand already; (b) the teacher considered an explanation to be too complex, either for the children to understand or for herself to formulate; (c) the teacher did not consider it important for the children to get this bit right — whether or not this was the case it could be construed as such by the children; (d) the teacher did not have an explanation herself.

Explanations were not offered for a number of items. Without wishing to suggest that explanations could or should always be given, it is interesting with hindsight to consider some possible questions the children might have had. For example, no explanation is given for 'Friday' having a capital 'F'. It is likely that names of days of the week have been cited in the past as always requiring capital letters, but on this occasion the appearance of a capital letter might have seemed arbitrary.

There is also no explanation for the full stops in:

On Friday I went to a bonfire. It was a huge bonfire.

This construction could appear particularly confusing in the light of the later statement, referring to the full stop after 'night sky': 'I've finished telling you about the bonfire now so I'll put a full stop'. The suggestion that full stops are used to separate subjects — repeated in the statement: 'I've finished talking about the firework now, so I've put a full stop' — is not borne out by the insertion of a full stop between two sentences about the same subject, as in, 'On Friday I went to a bonfire. It was a huge bonfire.'

Kress (1982) suggests that children's difficulties with punctuation largely arise from the fact that 'Perhaps the major part of learning to write consists in the mastery of the linguistic unit of sentence'(p. 70). Therefore, while the move from one subject to another might constitute a form of reasoning children can understand, the notion of separating two or more sentences which refer to the same subject is a far more complex one. As Kress points out, 'the early writing of children is characterised by the absence of the sentence'. If full stops are used, they are likely to be used to separate more easily understood units such as lines, pages, or subjects (see also Edelsky, 1983).

What knowledge are the children assumed to have?

Terms used by the teacher here include 'begin', 'name', 'full stop', 'capital letter', 'exclamation mark'. Perhaps surprisingly for the context in which this event is presented, the term 'sentence' is not used. The use of the terms 'begin' and 'name' have been discussed above, and it has been suggested that even these terms are not devoid of ambiguity. The other terms are used only in the context of talking about language, and children's knowledge of this metalanguage has been the subject of a recognised body of research.

For example, Downing (1970; 1976), Reid (1966; 1983) and Ferreiro & Teberosky (1982) have all demonstrated that children are often confused by terms such as 'word', 'letter', 'sentence', 'line'. My own research has corroborated these findings. One boy in this class, who consistently seems to put full stops at the end of every line, told me they are to show 'the end of the story'. On this occasion he wrote:

on bonfire night I had a fire in me
bakc garden.
And I had fire works it was fun.
And I had sparklers they were fun.
but me dad said it is bed tame.

In this instance his use of full stops suggests he is using them for a change of subject, as outlined above — indeed, he has adjusted his line lengths to suit his statements. On a different occasion, however, three months later, he wrote:

Oune upon a time.
A man went back.
in time and he went.
To Jrassik Parkc.
he saw a dinosaur.
it was a T-rex.

This time it is less easy to determine any other reasoning behind his use of full stops than that they go at the ends of lines. On both occasions he said his full stops were for 'the end of the story'. In the first instance he appears to be substituting 'story' for 'sentence', and in the second by 'story' he seems to mean 'line'. Certainly there is a common confusion between the terms 'sentence' and 'line', which can perhaps account for many children's use of end-line full stops: they can justify this by saying they have put full stops at the ends of sentences. (Incidentally, such errors are not helped by children's story books which often consist of one sentence per line.)

My point here is that children are often unclear about the meanings of terms to do with literacy and sometimes so are teachers. If children are not clear about the meanings of terms used by the teacher, or the terms used in explanations, it seems they will inevitably be, to some extent, left formulating their own hypotheses about the meanings of the rules and terminology.

There is also apparent confusion prevalent amongst young children about the difference between capital letters and small letters. It is very common to see children at the age of six or seven writing with a seemingly haphazard combination of upper and lower case letters. One of the children on this day wrote:

> on my hoLerday I went to
> The Bonfire and I haD a
> ToryapuLe and it was yum.

Through talking to children as they write I have found that, in addition to the problem of remembering which way round 'b's and 'd's and 'p's and 'q's should go, children also forget whether 'p's, 'f's, 'g's, 'j's and so on, go above or below the line. This results in many of these letters looking like capitals when they are not intended to be. The example above also shows capital 'T's, 'D's and 'L's in the middle of a text. When asked about this, the child agreed that they are capital letters, but did not see fit to alter them. An extreme example of this kind of behaviour was one very bright six-year-old boy who wrote:

> Bean B has SOME SOIL BUT WE ARE going to do nothing to it.

This was clearly a deliberate use of capital letters, but appears not to be used to show emphasis. When I asked him about it, the boy said, 'I just wanted to see if I could do it.' Such examples suggest that children's writing does not necessarily reflect either their intentions — in that a letter might look like a capital when it was intended to be lower case — or their real knowledge. For example, they might be experimenting, or it might be that they see no real reason for sticking to the rules they have learnt.

On the other hand, it is easy to assume that children have learnt which letters are capital and which are not when really they are unclear of the difference, or of which is which. It is not uncommon to hear children of this age say, for example, 'How does a capital "K" go again?' From my own research it seems that if a child aged five to seven is presented with a text and asked to point out the capital letters, the child will often indicate lower case letters such as 'f', 'w' and 'm', and offer the explanation that 'They're big.' When using a text containing a typewritten 'g' with which the children were not familiar, this letter was included with the letters regarded as capitals. This suggests, in contrast to the paragraph above, that knowledge of capital and lower case letters is often far from complete. This could then make problematic the instruction, 'Put a capital letter at the beginning.'

The significance of these observations is that if a child thinks, for instance, that 'w' is a capital letter and 'N' is a small letter, then their use of these letters will be consistently wrong in adult terms, even though the child might consider itself to be following the teacher's instructions. Thus the child might understand the principle, but appear to misapply it. It is therefore important to consider the possibility that children's interpretations of terms used by the teacher might not match the adult's understanding.

What do the children appear to know about punctuation?

This question can be posed in two different ways:

(i) What do the children appear to know about punctuation from what they say in response to the teacher?

(ii) What do the children appear to know about punctuation from what they write?

(i) The episode itself suggests that the children are able to recite rules to do with capital letters and full stops. These rules are not based on the concept of sentence, but on the simpler concept of one thing following another, or a capital letter being used for a name. However, one child demonstrates some understanding of the concept of sentence, pointing out the need for a full stop in what the teacher has written. The children's suggestions for a term to describe the exclamation mark suggest they have knowledge of at least the names of other punctuation marks — commas and question marks. When the name 'exclamation mark' is given, some of the children indicate recognition of the term.

(ii) It might be supposed that the writing produced by the children immediately following this event reflects their knowledge of punctuation. As the research carried out by Calkins (1980) has pointed out, however, learning rules for punctuation is not the same as applying them in free writing. Almost all of these children would have been able to cite the rule that a full stop follows a capital letter, or that a capital letter is used for a name. The incidence of these rules being applied, however, was low. One example is:

on My holiday's I went to christpher's party.

we playD Sleeping Lions and Lena Wun
Kath's sister then musicle chairs. and Amy
Wun that Game then We had a happy Meal I
got a dinasor we all got the Same then We
playD With them then the LaDy give a McFunBox
it Was ace it had a dice we made it then
Me and My Sister playD a game.

Also of interest in this example is the scarcity of full stops, but more striking still is the fact that many children do not use full stops at all. For example one child wrote two pages of text. The only full stop appeared at the end of the first page:

...and
we sor a moth brit won.

The second page begins:

and Iy went to bed and...

This child's writing displayed the common strategy of using connectives such as 'and' or 'because' rather than full stops. It is notable, however, that even without a connective she did not use a full stop, as in 'we sor a luving fawrwakc Iy had some frood we had chops...'. This suggests that, although her one full stop seems to fit the same pattern as the previous child, following a full stop with a lower case 'and', the main factor influencing its use was that it occurred at the end of the page.

It is interesting to see whether or not the child who pointed out the teacher's punctuation error, thereby appearing to show some grammatical sense before the event, produced grammatical sentences herself. She wrote:

On my holday I had a
bonFyer . I had thar spacekls
we had a toFeappels at
The bonfaye. we set oFF a
roceta. and FayerWecs . [and] ['and' has been crossed out by the child]
my Frends ceame with me.
my frends were cold Haner and
gesecar . and my frend Hane
was scard at the bonfire.

This writing is immediately striking in comparison with the majority of texts produced for the number of full stops included. This child at times uses a full stop in conjunction with, rather than instead of, a connective, but the fact that she has crossed out one of her 'and's suggests a recognition that this is an error. She has omitted a full stop after 'spacekls', although this could be attributed to the fact that the end of the sentence left no room at the side of the page for a full stop. The extra full stop after 'roceta' could also be explained by regarding the 'and Fayerwecs' as an afterthought.

The writing produced by another child exhibits different characteristics. Like the examples above, connectives are used, but this child manages to capitalise them when they follow a full stop:

> On Friday I went to the caste to see
> the bonefire. And I saw the Firewrok's
> and they were different colours.
> And it was good Fun and I had a
> toffee apple and some sparcels
> and I had some Firewrork's in my
> garden and it went bang! I
> like boneFire night it is good Fun

Only one child on this occasion produced grammatically correct sentences. In other writing produced around this time he also showed competent use of speech marks, apostrophes and question marks. However, when asked how he knew where to put his full stops, he replied, 'I don't know — I just did it.' It seems to me that this child has achieved the intuitive sense of sentences described by Wilde (1988) and Cordeiro (1988). If we, as mature and fluent writers, were asked how we decided where to put full stops many would probably reply, 'I don't know — I just did it.'

Of course, the type of event described in this chapter may not be the only experience children have of punctuation being taught. During the writing process itself the majority of requests for help from the children were for spellings. I did not witness any exchanges to do with punctuation, apart from those initiated by myself. After the children had finished their work it was marked by the teacher. Typically her marking consisted of: ticking next to one or two of a child's full stops; writing one or two spellings over the top of the child's attempts; crossing out the word 'and' when it followed a full stop and capitalising the first letter of the next word; and writing a positive comment or question at the end of the writing.

Many pieces of writing were given fewer ticks — partly, it seems, because many contained fewer full stops. It was not the teacher's practice to insert punctuation marks, but she did sometimes delete unnecessary 'and's. The placing of ticks next to full stops and the deletion of connectives is presumably intended to reinforce the importance of writing in sentences. The teacher did not, however, believe in excessive corrections on children's writing. The question of effective marking is, of course, another issue in itself, and there can be no certainty that correcting a young child's errors will lead to that child correcting its own errors in the future (see Perera, 1985, on marking children's writing).

Conclusion

The central focus of this chapter has been one event in the life of a Year 2 class and their teacher, which in total (including the children writing) occupied less than one hour of a school day. Although it might therefore appear to be insignificant as a learning episode, its importance lies in its very 'everydayness'; it is clear from the children's ritualistic responses to questions that this was not a one-off event. Nevertheless, it would be misleading to suggest that writing was always approached in this way — the teacher giving the children her own 'news' was just one method used as a stimulus for a writing activity.

Through an analysis of various aspects of the incident, my intention has been both to recognise the difficulties faced by teachers trying to convey the basics of punctuation, and to identify some of the possible ambiguities as perceived by the children. Of course, such a deconstruction is possible with the benefit of hindsight, and, like Ivanic (1988), I am guilty of being unable to offer sensible alternatives. Indeed, it seems to me that the overwhelming question I am left with, is the one with which I began: 'How can young children be taught punctuation?' Given the complexities of the concepts involved in using punctuation, how can young children be aided in grasping an understanding of it?

Despite being unable to answer the above questions, it seems likely that the majority of the children in this class will, in time, achieve a better understanding of punctuation and will eventually deploy it 'intuitively' as they write. In the meantime it seems that as teachers we can only attempt to understand children's efforts and to facilitate them in the process of learning to use punctuation. It seems likely that, as suggested by Bennett et al. (1984) and Cordeiro, Cazden & Giacobbe (1983), the process cannot, and indeed should not, be forced. If children begin to feel — in the same way that reading can be seen as 'just letters' — that writing is 'just spelling and full stops', then they are unlikely to feel inclined to persevere. If learning to write in sentences is indeed a matter of acquiring an intuitive sense, then the more experience a child has with writing continuous prose, the more hope there is of achieving it. Finally, if more were known about children learning punctuation, perhaps less simplistic and specific demands would be made of those required to teach it. Perhaps then teachers might be allowed to concentrate on instilling an enthusiasm and love for language, which would in itself lead to an understanding of the mysteries of punctuation.

7 A Young Deaf Child Explores Punctuation

NADEEN T. RUIZ

Introduction

For several years I have studied the literacy development of my daughter, Elena, who is deaf. In two earlier studies I looked at her spelling and her reading (Ruiz, in press; Ruiz, in preparation). In both of theses studies I found that although Elena relied very minimally on sound-based strategies for spelling and reading and maximally on visual-based strategies, she has been an accelerated reader and speller. Elena began independently reading simple picture books at the end of her kindergarten year (age 6.3) and chapter books as she began second grade (age 7.6). During a recent evaluation of her reading, a teacher found that Elena could read and accurately retell the last story in the fifth-grade reader when she was only finishing her third-grade year (age 9.2). In regard to spelling, at the beginning of third grade (age 8.7) on a group, standardised test administered to all public school children (and not normed on deaf children), Elena scored better than 90% of the hearing children in the national sample.

My essential point in those previous studies was that some people's theories of how children learn to read and write need to be modified. Researchers who over-emphasise the role of sound (as embodied in intensive phonemic awareness and phonics instruction) in literacy development need to reconsider that role if profoundly deaf children from rich language and literacy environments can read and write well. Researchers who stress a single path to learning to read and write, again, a path that heavily depends on the decoding and encoding of sounds, need to widen their view to encompass the multiple ways children, both deaf and hearing, can become expert readers and writers.

In this chapter I look at how Elena has explored punctuation while writing for a variety of purposes in both the home and school setting from ages 3–9 years. My goals in this study are two-fold: (1) to examine whether Elena's data lend support to current theories or explanations of the development of punctuation, and (2) to raise further questions for those who study this area of literacy development.

Background

Deaf children with frequent opportunities to interact with others in literacy events develop working hypotheses about the forms and functions of print. They also become proficient readers and writers (Rottenberg, 1992; Ruiz, in press; Williams, 1991). As such, looking closely at how deaf children go about forming and using their hypotheses can help us understand what is fundamental to these complex processes associated with learning to read and write. They can also inform us about what is expendable.

So far, in the research with young deaf children that looks closely and longitudinally at their reading and writing, we see that what is fundamental to becoming literate is that: (a) deaf children are active language-users, a skill that often has been fostered in homes where parents and other family members use sign language, either because it is their native language (in the case of deaf family members), or because they have learned it as a second language or code (in the case of hearing parents — my own case); (b) deaf children see and tell stories through sign language; (c) deaf children have books and other forms of print signed and explained to them, and then eventually read these print forms to others; and (d) deaf children write often and for a wide range of purposes. Perusing this pared-down and very basic list, it is obvious that the theories of literacy development espoused by Ken Goodman, Frank Smith, Elizabeth Sulzby and others who stress the socially-interactive and meaning-centred aspects of learning to read and write can encompass and explain how deaf children can become proficient readers and writers.

On the other hand, this same research with deaf children has clearly told us what is expendable in our theories of literacy development: hearing, to any great degree. Consequently, theories of literacy development holding that letter–sound relationships must be 'overlearned' in order to read fluently, that phonemic awareness skills such as rhyming are crucial to reading, and that extensive sound-based encoding strategies are essential to spelling, are impaired.

Turning to an under-researched area of literacy development — punctuation — we find that discussions regarding the role of sound have also surfaced. They have often centred around the importance of intonation patterns as clues to when, for example, to use a period or comma versus the importance of morphosyntactic (grammar-based) clues. In this chapter I will keep these discussions in mind. Specifically, my main related question is: How far can a largely visual, meaning-based approach to punctuation (Elena's approach as a deaf child, and potentially other children's approaches) get you on the way to becoming proficient at punctuating? If it can get you to where hearing children arrive in punctuation development, then once again explanations that depend too heavily on sound/intonation aspects may need rethinking.

Another question regarding punctuation emerges from the work of an international leader in the field of early literacy development, Emilia Ferreiro. Recently Ferreiro has posited an interesting relationship between sound-related aspects of writing and punctuation. In a review of her seminal work in the area of early literacy development Ferreiro mentions that when hearing children writing in an alphabetic language begin to initially and intensively concentrate on the phonemic aspects of writing (the alphabetic period) they do not focus on other aspects of writing — the 'non-alphabetic aspects,' such as word segmentation, punctuation marks, and capitalisation, among others (Ferreiro, 1991: 8). But what happens when children do not intensively concentrate on sound–symbol relationships? In Elena's case she did not go through the syllabic or alphabetic periods in learning to spell that have been identified with hearing children (Ruiz, in press). This may mean that the inattention to punctuation noted by Ferreiro among children concentrating on encoding sounds does not occur among children concentrating on visual strategies for spelling. So another working question as we look at Elena's writing is: Are children who follow a largely visual, meaning-based approach to spelling (Elena's approach as a deaf child, and potentially other children's approaches) more consistent punctuators? If the answer is yes, this relationship between punctuation and spelling may signal theoretical grounds for combining discussions of punctuation and spelling, rather than simply traditionally doing so. Furthermore, in the classroom teachers may use this information to understand that beginning phonemic spellers, seemingly 'behind' more visual spellers in terms of punctuation, will attend to those 'nonalphabetic' details later in their writing.

I used a case study approach to following Elena's acquisition of punctuation in her writing. The majority of written products I used for analysis are pieces of writing that she initiated at home and did independently. I also reviewed any extended pieces of text that her teachers sent home in the first through third grades, ages 6 to 9 years. Finally, I administered the punctuation section of the *Concepts About Print Test* (Clay,

1993) at the end of her kindergarten year (age 6.3) and an adapted version as she began fourth grade (age 9.5).

When Elena was deafened at just over one year old, our family needed to choose a sign language system to communicate with her. One option at that time was *American Sign Language* (ASL), a language in its own right, with its own syntax, lexicon, morphology and pragmatics. The other option was *Signed English*, a system created principally by educators to manually encode the English language as much as possible. Given my professional background in bilingual education — a field which has shown repeatedly that children achieve better in both their first and second languages when parents retain and use their first language at home with their children — our family chose to use Signed English. We did not choose to learn an entirely new language to communicate with our daughter; English, along with Spanish, is a language my husband and I speak fluently. (See Ruiz, in press, for additional details of Elena's language background.)

Signed English does have ways to mark periods, question marks, exclamation marks, apostrophes, commas and ellipses. All of these signs are marked by drawing them in the space in front of one's body, e.g., the sign for period is simply miming the placement of a dot in the air with one's index finger. The exceptions are possessive apostrophes and some contractive apostrophes which are cases I'll take up a bit later. However, in normal conversation that is not explicitly about writing conventions, we follow the oral English pattern of not marking these forms of punctuation in our everyday signing. For example, signers of Signed English do not sign 'period' at the end of their sentences, just as speakers of English do not say 'period' when they finish theirs. I do, however, occasionally sign a question mark after I ask Elena a question. I imagine I do that to signal that I need her to respond. With hearing children, intonation, semantics, syntax, pragmatics and perhaps some facial expression signal contingent queries. With children with a profound hearing loss such as Elena, especially if they are not wearing hearing aids at the time or are out of range to receive auditory information, intonation is not a recourse. That may be the reason for my spontaneous but intermittent signing of question marks in everyday conversation.

We do more or less consistently mark possessive apostrophes, 's,' and we distinguish them from the simple plural 's.' The plural 's' is marked in Signed English by forming the manual sign for 's' (a fist) and twisting it slightly out from the body, e.g., to the right if one is right-handed. In contrast, the possessive apostrophe is marked with a slight inward turn of the fist, e.g. to the left if one is right-handed.

Contractive apostrophes take two forms. The common contractions of *can't, don't* and *won't* are signed with three separate signs that do not overtly mark the apostrophe (e.g. *won't* is signed with a thumb jerked backwards over the shoulder). All other contractions (*doesn't, hasn't, mustn't*) are signed with the manual letter 'n' twisted inwards to the body.

With regard to the final aspect of punctuation considered in this study, sentence segmentation, we more or less use intonation patterns when we sign, including pause time, similar to parents communicating only orally, although these relationships are probably as variable as they are in spoken language. In all honesty, however, we speak more slowly when we talk to Elena because we are simultaneously signing. This is especially true of my husband who is less fluent in sign language than I am.

For the most part, I gave no instruction to Elena about how to use punctuation in her writing. My goal with her has always been to encourage literacy risk-taking. So, for example, when Elena wrote a comment on the class-created Big Book that she brought home from kindergarten at age 6.2, *I eanazy Thzp Book TaSS I loYQ TaZZ Watana WOS I WTAR OR K XXXX XXXXXXXXXXX Elena,* I did not correct her spelling or punctuation. With an unintelligible message as in this case, I simply asked her to 'read' it to me which she did in the following way: 'I enjoyed this book that I love. That. What. Was. I. Or, kiss, kiss, kiss,' (etc.). I always attempted to react to her intended meaning and not to her writing mechanics.

There were only a few exceptions to my *laissez-faire* policy to punctuation. First, I helped Elena edit about three books that she drafted at home during her first and second-grade years (ages 6 to 8). Also, during her third-grade year (ages 8 to 9) I helped her edit the twice-weekly homework assignment of writing sentences and 'stories' with her spelling words. Those editing sessions included discussions of periods, quotation marks, commas for setting off quotations, and capitalisation.

As far as direct instruction on punctuation at school, I rely on my background in classroom teaching, research and teacher-training to categorise Elena's schooling as providing relatively little. Her school has taken initial steps to becoming a whole-language school (Edelsky, Altwerger & Flores, 1991) by de-emphasising or eliminating the spelling and language arts workbooks. Unfortunately, however, they have not taken the steps of consistently teaching skills within authentic contexts.

Things began relatively well in kindergarten and first grade. Her kindergarten teacher did a daily demonstration of writing by recording a dictated message from a child a day on a large sheet of paper in front of the class. In first grade, the teacher gave the students frequent opportunities to write in journals (which often she or Elena's sign-language interpreter responded to in writing). The teacher also encouraged Elena and her classmates to draft stories. She did not give mini-lessons on punctuation and edited only one story for publication.

In second grade, there was no direct instruction of punctuation. For the first half of third grade this was also true until the teacher began Writers Workshop (Graves, 1983). Though the teacher did not provide class mini-lessons, she allowed Elena the opportunity to publish three books, all of which involved editing with an adult.

Elena's Punctuation Development

This discussion describes Elena's growing use of and knowledge about word and sentence segmentation, periods, question marks, exclamation marks, commas, apostrophes and ellipses. I focus on her development during her kindergarten and first-grade years. This allows me to not only try and capture her early, dynamic attempts at punctuation but allows readers to compare her usage with what seems to be the most researched group of developing punctuators, first graders (Cordeiro, Giacobbe & Cazden, 1983).

Age 3–5.6 years: Preschool

After following a very predictable course through early scribble writing, contiguous drawing and writing, and differentiated drawing and writing (as in labels), Elena began to write series of words when she turned five and was in pre-school. These words were either a few memorised, conventionally spelled words such as family names, or spellings that she generated (letter strings: series of letters with little or no relation to the conventional spellings). For the most part she segmented these words by writing them in list-like format. This list-like format (lots of margin space to the right of the words) persisted a long while through Elena's writing, through age 6.

In general, Elena did not use punctuation marks in her scribbling and writing during this period. Only twice in a dialogue journal we did at home during summer vacation before kindergarten (age 5.4) did Elena experiment with some periods between words (*no .KAZgo .ARES.vnbh.phae*), a way of segmenting found by other researchers of hearing children (Edelsky, 1983).

Age 5.6–6.6 years: Kindergarten

As Elena began kindergarten, she also began a period of great experi-

Example 7.1

mentation with punctuation and text in general. At this point she branched out from list-like text to text flowing left to right, but did not segment words or sentences. For example, writing of her (temporary) heroine she produced: *IloveMadonna*.

Also at this time I found Elena's first spontaneous use of periods for something other than individual word segmentation. She used them in a note she delivered to me after she became very frustrated playing softball. Example 7.1 is this note which she informed me to say, 'I'm so mad at you!' She read this to me fiercely and loudly, in a style calling conventionally for an exclamation mark. Interestingly there are two periods in this note, both floating above the line as almost a year before in her dialogue journal, as well as a angry-looking face. It seems at this point that to depict the emphatic tone of her message Elena certainly used drawing, but was also beginning to use some sort of conventional punctuation, i.e. the two periods. The exclamation mark was not yet in her repertoire. After this piece, Elena did not use periods again until much later in her kindergarten year, about six months from this time.

For almost three-quarters of her kindergarten year, Elena used only one

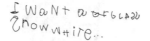

Example 7.2

punctuation convention, but a rather surprising one: the ellipsis. Before Christmas of this year, Elena made about 15 catalogue-like books, often titled *Toy Books*, that had as one of their functions to tell us what she wanted to receive as gifts. In those books, Elena began to frequently use the ellipsis more or less appropriately, that is, signalling very accurately that more requests were to come: *I want a buggy…* (Example 7.2).

For this same period, Elena did not use: (a) possessive apostrophes (*Elena's birthday*) except once while copying a book title, (b) contractive apostrophes, (c) periods, (d) question marks, (e) exclamation marks, (f) commas, nor (g) consistent capitalisation. Word and sentence segmentation were not consistently apparent either. This may be because Elena produced few extended texts at this time (with multiple sentences), and when she did

TOMOLLY

ELENa

FROM

~~Elor~~

MARCH

~~(drawing)~~

YOU
R

NOT.
COMING

TO
MY

~~HOUSE~~ HOU2E

BUT
YOU
R
COMING
TO NELLIE2
HOUZE

FOR A
PARTY

Example 7.3

produce extended text with spellings often solicited from adults, it retained the list-like format (Example 7.3). In this latter context of near-by, helping adults, Elena tended to segment words more often than when she wrote independently.

Right before Elena's sixth birthday during her kindergarten year, there was a small explosion of writing, similar to the Christmas catalogue frenzy, as she planned and imagined her birthday. Three other punctuation conventions emerged next, but again, ones not easily predicted as appearing first in children's writing: the hyphen, the tilde (ñ) (a writing convention used in Spanish) and a narrow use of the question mark. She used the hyphen for writing phone numbers, for writing the word 'birth-day' as she had seen written on a book title, and for segmenting between the names of girls that she wanted to invite to her sixth birthday party. She also used the tilde correctly as she copied the word *'piñata'* for a book she wrote anticipating the activities at her birthday party, but overextended its use on a subsequent page (Examples 7.4a and 7.4b). Finally, Elena began to use the question mark in phrases such as *I want a ?* and *Elena is ?* At this point the question mark seemed to function as a stand-in for 'take a guess.'

Soon after this period of intensive writing at home, Elena began to incorporate more punctuation marks in her writing. A very sparse sprinkling of periods emerged, this time not floating above the line, but still used as word segmentation in short texts (*Mollys.car.* and *Magics.Books*). Her usage of the question mark as 'guess what/who' continued, but for the first time expanded to mark an interrogative: *Do you love me?* This latter use was very sporadic, however.

Her still-developing concepts about question marks were apparent in her responses to the *Concepts About Print Test* that I gave Elena during this time. When I asked what the question mark was for during this test, Elena replied, 'When you don't know someone's name you put it over there,' confirming the 'guess what/who' function suggested in her writing products. To the question regarding a period, Elena responded, 'If something is long you put a period on it.' With the comma, she stated, 'This is for something short.' Regarding quotation marks, she reported, 'These are for if they're too long.' Elena was unable to show me a capital letter.

Not long after this, however, after a few weeks of doing a summer dialogue journal with my husband and me and her baby-sitters, Elena used her first question mark in extended, non-formulaic text. She also threw in lots of exclamation marks for the emphatic tone she sought in this message regarding her feelings for our new puppy (Example 7.5).

In summary, Elena went from very little punctuation in her writing to a substantial increase. Her first-acquired punctuation marks were not those listed in many kindergarten or first-grade teachers class objectives: the ellipsis, the hyphen, and the tilde. But they were very tied to the things she was excited about writing, specifically, personalised toy-catalogues and birthday-associated texts (primarily books and invitations).

One other finding beyond the scope of this chapter needs to be briefly mentioned. As I examine Elena's writing during this period for the

Example 7.4a

Example 7.4b

> Do you like your new puppy? He
> sure does sleep a lot. It is too hot
> to take him outside, maybe when
> it is not so hot we will take
> him for a walk.

> ΓΥΓΥΓ/2E!

> I DO! I love Ti

> WHX Teh Puppk 2aTP.
> Lor r
> I do not know why he sleeps
> a lot. Probably because he is
> only a baby.

Example 7.5

punctuation signs I mentioned in the beginning, I miss out on a lot of 'non-alphabetic' (Ferreiro, 1991) work that Elena is undertaking. For example, in various books, letters and socio-dramatic play props written at home, Elena proficiently used cartoon bubbles to frame her character's speech, variations on those bubbles to indicate that her characters were engaging in inner speech, questions with boxes provided for the audience's response (*I want you to love me? Yse ro no*), and check marks and x's to signal items on lists. She also experimented with Chinese character-writing, with pretend money-making, and with 'punctuation' in number sentences (*1l = 4; 2 + 1 - 8*, etc.). These may not be punctuation signs or text format conventions on the *Concepts About Print Test*, but they were all non-alphabetic ways Elena showed herself and others that she was a prolific, interesting writer.

Ages 6.6–7.6: First grade

In Elena's writing at home this year she used a wide range of punctuation forms. She continued to play with the ellipsis in messages, such as *grrr...*, *hmmm...*, *but...*, and *duh...* (The latter she teasingly wrote on the outside of a birthday card to her father after asking me what 'duh' meant in a comic book she was reading.) The over-extended tilde popped up only once during this period, and then faded away to come back much later in third grade and used appropriately on a word in Spanish. The hyphen was largely unused except for an early form of 'you're' as *you-re*.

Elena now used question marks to appropriately mark interrogative forms. She began to use periods more consistently, especially when writing at home where she was largely in control of purposes and times for writing. (Her story drafts from first grade looked rushed, and without a lot of detail in drawing or length of text. They largely had drawings and one-word labels, and did not have periods, except two very different-looking books written at the end of the year, seemingly with a lot more care.) Periods for initials, for after numerals in lists, and for abbreviations of months while writing dates she used very accurately. Elena also used exclamation marks very consistently and appropriately at this time.

New punctuation marks that emerged during this period were parentheses, e.g. in a book title written at home: *My First Sewing Dresses (Fancy Dresses)* and in a 'Wanted Poster' that she devised for her older brother (Example 7.6). In that same figure we can see that Elena began using commas, but only for numbers as in the poster, or for writing the date in

Example 7.6

other pieces, until the very end of this time period. Elena also used the colon for writing the hour.

Contractive forms of words were very dynamic in Elena's repertoire during this time. At the beginning of her first-grade year she began to use *n'* for 'and' as in *David n' me* and *He say he likes me n' my toys*. Around this same time also Elena wrote *m'* for 'I'm' a number of times, a fairly reasonable extension of the more conventional process she followed with 'and' and n'. She also began to experiment with 'don't': in the previous period she tried to represent 'don't' with a letter string, *donno*, but now it became variously *dnot'*, and *dot'n*, until finally stabilising at *don't* at the end of this period. *Can't* appeared in March of this year and also stabilised.

In terms of the possessive apostrophe, Elena went from omitting it to consistently using it appropriately. Elena wrote a book when she had finished first grade and was about to enter second. This was a book that she initiated at home and wrote independently. In it we had: correct usage of word segmentation, exclamation marks and question marks; sporadic use of periods; overuse of the comma for marking quotations; and an initial attempt at using quotation marks.

Ages 7.6–8.6: Second grade

While in second grade, Elena's use of periods increased. In the first page of a book she wrote at home about a good friend in November of her second-grade year, she wrote:

> *Katie is my Best Friend in the world. We never aruge. because we are Best Bubbies. That's why we never aruge. We go to our houses. We love Sweet Valley kids and Twins Books.*

Later in this book Elena shows that she's still working on punctuation marks that she needs to depict a series of items:

> *We have a club called the Jumpers. or girl Talks.or gostwriters.*

Soon after this book, however, Elena used the comma to correctly differentiate a series in, not surprisingly, her Christmas lists of this year. After initially misusing the comma in closing letter salutations, as in one of her letters to, at that time, President-elect Clinton, *love, your, friend Elena,* she soon began to use them conventionally.

During her second-grade year, Elena stabilised her use of possessive (*my brother's birthday*) and contractive apostrophes (*she's* for 'she is'), with only one over-extension among the data to *my's* for 'mine.' She also used the hyphen for the first time to separate a word when she came to the end of

6/3/93

Dear Bill   I'm sorry
that I didn't write to
you because I have
tons of homework. And I'm
And its past my birthday
and I got two things
from my mom and dad
I got a doil that cost
$91.00   and I made
my First holy commuin
I got alot of money.
do you Know my wish?
it is People — to stop
taking drugs I hate drugs

because a bad man
threwed a pin at
my best friend Katie
right here near the
eye.   And now
She a little mark
on her alead. this
is a Picure of my
brother
and my
doll ↓

p.s I'm going
to Washingtion D.c.!
meer me
near
house your
P.s.s.
I don't

Knoa
When.

Example 7.7

the line, using it correctly, *sing -ing*. She also used the hyphen during socio-dramatic play to invent a name of a delivery company, *Devl-a Want*.

As example of her punctuation near the end of this period I include a letter that she wrote to President Bill Clinton (Example 7.7). Notice the still sporadic, but improved use of periods, her rhetorical use of the question mark, correctly contracted forms such as *didn't*, and the attempt at distinguishing between two consecutive postscripts on the envelope.

Ages 8.6–9.6: Third grade

During this past year, Elena has continued to refine her punctuation. In October she was administered an achievement test with a national sample (of hearing children) and scored at the 63rd percentile for language mechanics.

This progress is most evident in her writing of the longer text she was relatively infrequently asked to produce in her classroom, and in her self-initiated writing at home, now mostly letters to family members and others. A good place to observe this refinement and growing range of punctuation use are in two examples of her spontaneous use of quotation marks. In February of her third-grade year, Elena left the following note for me after I sent her to her room for throwing a stuffed animal:

> I'm really sorry. I just wanted to have fun. I'm sorry that I therw Misty saying' "I don't want your crummy cat!" I did that to get your _Antenttoin_. I wanted to do that. If you got my antenttoin I would say: "I love you."

In third grade she was writing stories which had generally correct use of capitalisation, sentence segmentation and segmentation marks, parentheses, hyphens, colons and quotations. Elena also began to show a greater range of uses for the comma, segmenting not only a series of items and ideas but also larger grammatical units within a sentence, as in the first sentence.

Elena and I recently sat and redid an adaptation of the punctuation section of the *Concepts about Print Test*. We used a children's chapter book instead of the test protocol, and I extended my questions about a greater range of punctuation marks. To all but one question she showed that she knew how to correctly use the punctuation signs, even in the one case where she forgot the English name (but not the manual sign) for quotation marks. All of these correct responses depended on their grammatical usage and not intonation.

The one punctuation mark whose function she could not supply was the comma. She correctly named it, but simply said with some embarrassment that she didn't know. A day after this conversation, I showed her the actual samples of her writing which illustrated the varied way she had used commas in her writing this past year, and asked her why she had used them. To commas used in delineating a series words or phrases she said:

> Because there won't be a lot of words. It's for a short way, instead of saying 'or' and 'or' and 'and' and 'and.'

To all other uses of commas in her own writing (setting off a elaborating phrase) Elena gave grammatical and sensible answers, in one case saying, '...if you didn't use a comma it would cause misunderstanding.' The one example of comma usage from a book that I used during this session caused her problems. The sentence read, 'of course not,' replied Lucie. 'Watch this.' Elena's hunch was that the comma signalled that there was more to come: 'Like if there wasn't a comma, it'd just be a period, and there would be no "watch this."' It is clear that at age nine and entering fourth grade, Elena is still working on when to appropriately use the troublesome comma. (Fortunately, many of us adults can rely on editors.)

Conclusions and Questions for Further Study

With regard to my first research question, this study of Elena's exploration of punctuation indicates that deafness does not get in the way of becoming a good punctuator, even when direct instruction in punctuation has been relatively infrequent. Consequently, theories of punctuation development which strongly rely on children hearing (intonation patterns, pause time) do not explain how profoundly deaf children as Elena learn to punctuate. It is true that children rely on a variety of cues to punctuate — pragmatic, semantic, morphosyntactic and sound-based (as do adults — see Ivanic, this volume). But just as Sulzby stated regarding initial reading, children need some knowledge of each to punctuate, not perfect knowledge of each cueing system (Sulzby, 1992).

There are, however, remaining aspects of the question that warrant consideration. First, without complete access to sound-based cues as hearing children have, how did Elena learn to punctuate? In this chapter I have only tracked the course of Elena's early punctuation attempts without specifically examining the 'how' of these attempts. More work, combining the data on her reading and other aspects of her writing, is necessary to get at that aspect in a more definitive way. But from this initial study we can glean a few directions the answer might take. For example, early demonstrations of writing through dialogue journals and other genres, especially at home, probably helped Elena learn punctuation conventions. In addition, my husband and I signed and read stories to Elena intensively until she took over reading to us and then began to read independently. Frank Smith has cited the importance of children's book authors in helping children read (Smith, 1992). This probably extends to punctuating. Children's books provide natural language and attractive, engaging story lines that invite children to construct meaning. Beyond the words themselves are the punctuation marks that may be more salient to children approaching reading with visual, meaning-based strategies instead of sound-based ones.

Finally, her pressing need to write at home for a variety of her own purposes (leading my husband to call her the 'literacy monster' when he could not find any of his pens, staplers, or other writing tools) sparked punctuation experimentation and growth. Throughout these literacy events we tried to make Elena a risk-taker with literacy — one whose focus was the message, one not held back by over-attention to mechanics, and one who learned standard conventions when the context dictated that they were important. In essence, it is these experiences, and not hearing, that are most likely to have led her to continually refine her hypotheses about punctuation.

At the same time, a limitation of this study needs attention. Our communication system with Elena calls for simultaneous talking as well as pause times and intonation patterns similar to spoken English. Though we do not know exactly how much auditory information Elena receives with a profound hearing loss in both ears, she may receive some. So continuing studies of punctuation development with other deaf children who exclusively use sign language (and not voice) to communicate will be important to undertake, to more completely examine the relationship between sound and punctuation.

The second question posed for this chapter had to do with whether Elena had a lull in her punctuation use as observed in hearing children working on sound-based strategies for spelling words (Ferreiro, 1991). At the risk of looking like I'm hedging this question, I ask the readers — teachers and researchers who have seen a broad range of punctuation development to decide whether there was a lull.

If as a reader you find a relative lull, we have to then re-examine Ferreiro's hypothesis that it is an intensive concentration on sound encoding that causes the lull. Elena is unable to intensively concentrate on sound. We need to generate other possible reasons behind the lack of attention to punctuation. On the other hand, if you find — as I suspect — that there was no lull, that Elena punctuated more than hearing children do at the early period of writing development, then it may be that other visual design and generative spellers will attend to punctuation more. Teachers keeping to antiquated lists of what first graders (and so on) should know with regard to punctuation could limit the range of forms and purposes to which these children (and others) put punctuation. But more than anything, the second question pushes us to look more closely at and to pose more questions regarding potential relationships between children's spelling and punctuation strategies.

When children with an obvious communication difference such as Elena become skilled language-users, they offer us an opportunity to examine the fundamental aspects of language and literacy development. Once we understand what is fundamentally true of literacy development we can then better concentrate on individual children's paths towards learning to read and write. Teachers and researchers of both groups — the communicatively different and those without a biological basis for a communication difficulty — would do well to more consistently engage in a dialogue about the development of early literacy.

Acknowledgement

This work in this chapter was supported in part by a grant from the California State Department of Education, Special Programs Branch titled 'The OLE Research and Dissemination Project.'

8 Who Says What? Learning to 'Read' the Punctuation of Direct Speech

KATHARINE PERERA

Introduction

Stories often contain direct speech — in fact, it's hard to imagine an adult novel without it. But it's an important part of children's stories too. We can think of the number of traditional stories in which the words of the characters not only form an essential element of the story but also appear, virtually unchanged, in numerous different versions — for example:

Who's been sleeping in *my* bed?

Fee fi fo fum, I smell the blood of an English man.

I'll huff and I'll puff and I'll blow your house down.

All the better to see you with, my dear.

Mirror, mirror on the wall, who's the fairest of them all?

Each of these utterances can be readily assigned to a well-known character.

Not surprisingly, many of children's earliest reading books include direct speech too. In fact, a study by Baker & Freebody (1989) of 163 books described as 'basal and supplementary readers' suggests that it occurs exceptionally frequently in this kind of material. They report that, taking occurrences of *said, say* and *says* together, this word family is second in frequency to *the* in their corpus of nearly 84,000 words. By way of comparison, they note that the *say* words don't figure at all in the 50 most common words in a corpus of the spoken English of American children aged 4;6 to 5;6. They comment, 'This indicates the extraordinary prevalence of the reportage of talk in these early school books' (p. 37).

The inclusion of direct speech can have two related benefits. The language given to characters to speak may be closer to the language that children actually use than the remainder of the text is, and — perhaps for that reason — young readers sometimes seem able to read it aloud with more involvement and expression. In a study of children's development in oral reading that I carried out over a three-year period, starting when they were aged 5 (Perera, 1989), I found that they would almost act out the parts when they read passages like this:

(1) Peter painted a picture
     of the king.
     But he didn't like it.
     "This is a silly picture,"
     he said.
     Pat looked at the picture.
     She laughed and laughed.
     "Stop laughing!" shouted Peter.
     "I can't stop," laughed Pat.
     "The king's face is so funny." (*Peter's Unhappy Day*)

The beneficial effect only applied when they could identify with the characters, though.

The disadvantage of direct speech is that the child has to be able to work out who is speaking and, if there is a change of speaker, recognise that too. This can be a difficult task. After a detailed analysis of a passage of direct speech in an early reading book, Baker & Freebody make this comment:

> We see then, how closely the text must be read to work out who said what to whom, and how dependent we are on the narrator, on punctuation and on culturally based inferences to cope with both regular and irregular formats. (pp. 129–30)

It is that dependence on punctuation which forms the subject of this chapter. After illustrating the surprisingly wide range of ways of presenting direct speech that young readers come across in their early reading books, I shall show how children begin to learn to 'read' the punctuation — i.e. not only to perceive and recognise the marks on the page but also to use them to work out who says what, so that they get the right meaning from the text.

The presence of direct speech is signalled by reporting clauses which attribute words to a speaker, and by punctuation and layout. The most obvious feature of punctuation that demarcates a stretch of direct speech is a pair of inverted commas; these co-occur with capitalisation, commas and sentence-final punctuation (full stops, question marks and exclamation marks).

In books for very young readers there is a surprising variety of ways in which direct speech is presented, with some reading schemes using different styles of presentation in earlier and later stages of the scheme. I will now illustrate something of the range of possibilities.

The Presentation of Direct Speech in Early Reading Schemes

Speech attribution

No reporting clauses

Some very early books don't use reporting clauses at all. There are four different ways in which non-attributed speech is presented. The text may be simply below or opposite the picture of the person assumed to be talking. For example, in Sally Grindley's *Knock Knock Who's There?* each piece of direct speech occurs opposite a picture of the speaker — either a young girl in bed or one of the creatures that people her frightening fantasies, e.g.

(2) Who's there?
     I'm a
     great big
     gorilla
     with fat furry arms
     and huge white teeth.

Where the speech of two or more characters is associated with a single picture, it may be necessary to look and read ahead in order to work out who is saying what, as in this extract from *Reading 360's Come for a Ride*:

(3) Can I go out to play, Mum?
     Can I go for a ride?
     Yes, you can
     but play in the park.
     Let's ride down here.
     No. Let's ride down here.
     We can go fast here.

Here, a young girl goes to the park with her friend, a boy. The words 'Let's ride down here' are printed below a picture of the two of them. It only becomes apparent that they must be spoken by the boy from the picture on the *next* page, which suggests that the response, 'No. Let's ride down here' comes from the girl.

Alternatively, the speech of different characters may be differentiated by the typeface, as in John Burningham's story *Granpa*, where the two characters are the grandfather and his granddaughter, whose words are printed in italics:

(4) If I catch a fish we can cook it for supper.
     What if you catch a whale, Granpa?

Another possibility is for the speech of different speakers to be marked off by sets of inverted commas, without any reporting clauses, as in this passage from *Shorty the Puppy, A New Home*:

(5) "Get out of my way!"
     "Quick, Jim!
     Get the puppy."

The first sentence is spoken by a rough-looking man, while the next two lines come from one of the boys.

The fourth possibility is for the speech to be enclosed in balloons, in the style of a comic strip. This is particularly common in series designed for home reading, e.g. *Longman Reading World, Read Along Stories* and *Read Together*. The balloon may be part of the illustration, and placed next to the character's face, or it may move out of the picture, positioning the text in a conventional arrangement below the illustration, as happens in the *Open Door* books.

Reporting clauses

Where there are reporting clauses, they can occur before, after or in the middle of the direct speech. As the following examples illustrate, regardless of whether the reporting clause is initial or final, it may be set out either on the same line as the direct speech (e.g. (6) and (8)) or on a separate line (e.g. (7) and (9)):

(6) They said, "He is playing a trick again." (*The Boy Who Cried Wolf*)
(7) His mother said,
     "Where's your yellow jumper, your new one?" (*Sammy's New Yellow Jumper*)
(8) "You must come to our castle," she said. (*The Broomstick Tree*)
(9) "It's still a bit big for me,"
     said Titch. (*You'll Soon Grow Into Them, Titch*)

Medial reporting clauses may be sandwiched within a character's speech, e.g.

(10) "I think," said Mother, "that Titch
     should have some new clothes." (*You'll Soon Grow Into Them, Titch*)

Here, the utterances on each side of the reporting clause are structurally incomplete, so it is clear that they belong together and that *said Mother* applies to both halves. In such cases it is normal for the reporting clause to be on the same line as the speech that it reports. In other instances, the reporting clause may end with a full stop and a line break and yet still be followed by the speech of the same character, e.g.

(11) "Grandmother is making cakes
      this morning," said Jennifer.
      "I will ask her for one, and
      you can put it on the black stepping-stone
      for the little old man." (*The Stepping Stones*)

The obvious problem is that there is no foolproof way of knowing at the start of the second sentence who is speaking, since the layout and punctuation can be just the same when there are two different speakers. In other words, we can't tell whether the reporting clause is medial, as it was in (11), or final, as in (12):

(12) "I always knew that you must never step
      on that black stepping-stone," said Roger.
      "Whitefoot went out again last night,"
      said Jennifer. (*The Stepping Stones*)

Both medial and final reporting clauses differ from initial clauses in allowing two possible orders for the subject and verb. These may occur in the normal statement order of subject plus verb, as in (8), *she said*, or in inverted verb–subject order, as in (9), (10), (11) and (12), e.g. *said Jennifer*. The examples illustrate the point that the subject–verb order is commonest when the subject is a pronoun such as *she* or *he* but the verb–subject order is the most usual when the subject is a noun or noun phrase such as *Jennifer*, *Mother*, *Titch*, *Roger*. It is possible for a pronoun to occur in the inverted order but it sounds particularly literary, e.g.

(13) "Just the thing for my lunch," said she. (*Mr McGee*)

In Table 8.1 I have set out the position and structure of 160 reporting clauses in 35 early reading books, with examples of each type. It is clear that final and medial reporting clauses are far more common than initial ones and, in those positions, inverted verb–subject clauses are more frequent than subject–verb ones.

Inverted commas

None

Some early reading books don't use inverted commas at all, presumably in the belief that they make life harder for the young reader. This is true of all the books that use speech balloons, which serve as a substitute for

Table 8.1 The position and structure of reporting clauses in 35 early reading books (N = 160)

Initial		Medial				Final			
SV		SV		VS		SV		VS	
Pro	N	Pro	N	Pro	N	Pro	N	Pro	N
He said	Tagg said	he called	Costas said	sang he	cried Billy	they snuffled	the King asked	said she	shouted the boy
7	11	11	6	1	40	16	9	1	58
		17		41		25		59	
18		58				84			

SV = subject verb; VS = verb subject; Pro = pronoun; N = noun

inverted commas, and also, for example, of the first three levels of *Ladybird*; of Level 3 of *Link-up* (1 and 2 don't contain any direct speech); of Levels 1–5 of *New Way*; of Level 4 of *Open Door* (1–3 use speech balloons); and of Levels 1 and 2 of *Reading 360*, with the exception of the last book in Level 2, where inverted commas are introduced for the first time. In most cases, the direct speech is set out just like the rest of the text, as in this example from a *New Way* story:

(14) Who made the shoes? asked his wife.
And who finished them?
asked the shoemaker?
They did not know. (*The Elves and the Shoemaker*)

But in *Link-up* it is indented, e.g.

(15) Then Jim said:
The little man is green now.
The policeman said:
Look out for traffic. (*Silly Children*)

Single inverted commas

A few reading schemes use single inverted commas, e.g. *Fuzzbuzz*, *Ginn Goes Home*, and *Oxford Reading Tree*:

(16) 'This way,' said Biff.
'No, this way,' said Chip. (*The Foggy Day*)

They are also used in a few of the very many non-scheme books in infant classrooms, e.g. *Mr McGee* and *Have You Seen the Crocodile?*

Double inverted commas

Most often when inverted commas are used, they are double. This is the case, for example, with *Bangers and Mash, Beacon Readers, Crown Readers, Headstart, Ladybird* (from Level 4), *Letterland, Link-up* (from Level 4), *Longman Reading World, New Way* (from Level 6), *One, Two, Three and Away, Open Door* (from Level 5), *Read Together* (from Level 4), *The Shorty Books, Story Chest,* and *Sunshine Books.*

Other punctuation

We can now consider what punctuation other than inverted commas conventionally occurs with direct speech.

Initial reporting clauses are followed by a comma. The direct speech then begins with a capital letter, e.g.

(17) Their mother said to them,
    "You are too big to live here any
    longer." (*The Three Little Pigs*)

It's clear that this constitutes an exception to the basic punctuation rule that the only words to begin with a capital letter are proper nouns and words that begin new sentences. However, the basic rule applies when the reporting clause is medial, since if that is punctuated with a comma, it is followed by a lower case letter, e.g.

(18) "Yes," the king said, "you must come with us." (*The Broomstick Tree*)

Final reporting clauses are followed by a full stop and are straightforward.

The situation is more complex, though, with regard to the punctuation of the direct speech itself when the reporting clause is medial or final. If the preceding direct speech is a statement or a command, then it generally ends with a comma rather than a full stop, e.g.

(19) "I am sailing to the dance feast in Suzan," he called out. (*Gnugu Lives in the Jungle*)

(20) "Let me keep him, Dad,"
    he said. (*Mark Fox*)

Predictably, the reporting clause begins with a lower case letter. In contrast, if the direct speech is a question or an exclamation, then it ends with a question mark or exclamation mark but is still followed by a lower case letter in the reporting clause:

(21) "Who could have made this footprint?"
    he asked. (*Robinson Crusoe*)

(22) 'Look at me!' he shouted down. (*Mr McGee*)

So, examples (21) and (22) are, like (17), exceptions to a basic punctuation rule because, in this case, sentence-final punctuation marks are not followed by a capital letter.

The examples from (17) to (22) illustrate conventional punctuation within direct speech. The early stages of some reading schemes are unconventional in using either reduced punctuation or none at all. For example, Level 2 of *New Way* uses full stops, commas and capital letters, but no question marks (or inverted commas, as we have already seen), e.g.

(23) Can I help you, said Ben.
    No, you can't, said Jip.

The first edition of *Link-up* (1972) didn't have capital letters (apart from proper nouns) in Levels 1–3 but, interestingly, these were restored to the revised 1986 edition. There is no punctuation at all in the early books of *Fuzzbuzz, Open Door, Reading 360* and *Through the Rainbow*, e.g.

(24) do you like
    my house
    yes
    may I come
    in your house
    no (*Open Door*)

This examination of the layout and punctuation of direct speech in early reading books suggests two things. First, if young children read books from a number of different sources, for example in an individualised approach (e.g. Moon, 1994), they may be meeting direct speech in rather varied guises. As skilled adult readers, we are so familiar with the functional equivalence between, say, single and double inverted commas that we probably don't normally notice which a particular book uses. Young readers, though, are still in the process of learning which minor differences of form are significant, such as the contrast between the letters 'b' and 'd' or 'h' and 'n', and which are irrelevant, such as the difference between 'a' and 'a' or 'g' and 'g', so we shouldn't assume that they can move unproblematically from one type of presentation to another.

Secondly, it becomes apparent that more clues about who is saying what are provided by some ways of presenting direct speech than by others. The next section examines this notion in more detail.

Informativeness of direct speech presentation

When any direct speech in a text comes from a single speaker, there is no real difficulty of attribution (although readers still have to be able to distinguish the character's words from the main narrative). The potentiality for confusion arises when there is a dialogue between two or more speakers. Crucially, it is necessary for a reader to know as early as possible when there has been a change of speaker. It's possible to illustrate a scale of informativeness by taking two utterances, the first spoken by speaker A and the second by speaker B, and looking to see how many clues that there has been a change of speaker are provided by different patterns of presentation.

I shall use variants of the two utterances in (25) to demonstrate a few of the many possible levels of informativeness.

(25) I can help
     the giant is hiding
     in a cave

As the speech is set out in (25), with no punctuation and no reporting clauses, it is maximally uninformative. In contrast, the version at (26) offers several clues to the speakers' identities:

(26) "I can help," said Jack.
     The princess said, 'The giant is
     hiding in a cave."

First, the inverted commas mark off the spoken words. Secondly, the reporting clause *said Jack* can only be medial or final; it can't be initial (and thereby signal a change of speaker) because initial reporting clauses can't have the inverted VS structure. Further, the comma after *help* serves to link the first utterance with the following reporting clause. Then the next reporting clause, *The princess said*, by being in initial position, gives the earliest possible warning that there is a change of speaker.

Between the two extremes of informativeness represented by (25) and (26), there is a wide range of other possibilities; one of these is set out at (27):

(27) "Can I help?"
     Jack said.
     "The giant is hiding
     in a cave,"
     Princess Petal said.
     "He is…"

In (27) the SV reporting clause *Jack said* could be final (as it is here), or medial if the next sentence was also spoken by Jack, or initial if it was signalling a change of speaker. The only feature which tells us that it is not initial in this example is the full stop rather than a comma after *said*; the question mark after *help* means that that sentence could end there, and the capital letter for *Jack* means that *Jack said* could introduce a new utterance. Similarly, the relationship between the second utterance and its reporting clause *Princess Petal said* is signalled only by the comma — rather than a full stop — after *cave*. This is because the capital letter which is needed for the proper noun *Princess Petal* could also be the marker of a new sentence. The very slight changes in punctuation which would alter the attribution of speech in (27) are shown in (28):

(28) "Can I help?"
    Jack said,
    "The giant is hiding
    in a cave."
    Princess Petal said,
    "He is…"

Now another speaker (who, we can assume, has been identified earlier) says, *Can I help?*, Jack says the second utterance and the princess the third. These examples also demonstrate that the very short lines favoured by some early reading books can be a positive disadvantage when they separate reporting clauses from the speech they report.

As a final example, we can see that (29) is slightly more informative than (27):

(29) "I can help,"
    he said.
    "The giant is hiding in a cave,"
    the princess said.

Here, the lower case letters for *he* and *the princess* provide an additional clue that the reporting clauses are final rather than initial.

What we need to know is whether young readers are, in fact, sensitive to some of these presentational details. In order to provide the beginnings of an answer to that question, I shall now describe a research study that I undertook with the aim of assessing children's responsiveness to various aspects of the direct speech they meet in their reading books.

Children's Responsiveness to the Presentation of Direct Speech

I became interested in young readers' responses to direct speech during the course of a longitudinal study of the development of fluency, rhythmicality and expressiveness in children's oral reading (Perera, 1989). Two things in particular caught my attention. First, even the youngest, weakest readers showed some sensitivity to punctuation. Secondly, a common oral reading error was for a reporting clause to be linked to the wrong stretch of speech, with the resulting misattribution often making baffling nonsense of the text. In order to illustrate these two findings, it is necessary first to give a very brief description of the longitudinal study.

The longitudinal study

Over the course of three years, I tape-recorded six children, individually, every three months as they read aloud from the book that they were currently using in the process of learning to read. I transcribed their reading and, by listening to each four seconds of tape over and over again on a loop-repeater tape recorder, I made a visual record of their intonation. Amongst other features, I noted which words were grouped together into 'chunks' (or *tone units*), which syllables were stressed, which was the most salient syllable in each tone unit, and what contour or 'tune' bound the words within the tone unit together. An adaptation of O'Connor & Arnold's (1973) intonational framework served as the basis of this record.

A problem that arises in writing about intonation is that it is necessary to try to represent on the page the tune and rhythm of the voice which are only partially captured by the conventional writing system. We all know that, in speech, the meaning of an utterance resides not in the words alone but in the way that they are said. So the phrase *Very clever* could be said with genuine admiration or with heavy sarcasm to mean the opposite. The written words alone cannot express these different meanings. Sometimes, especially with short simple utterances, punctuation can convey in writing something of what the tone of voice conveys in speech. So the words, *She won* can be punctuated in three different ways to reflect a matter-of-fact or excited or questioning pronunciation:

(30a) She won.

(30b) She won!

(30c) She won?

But, more often, the range of possible pronunciations (with their related meanings) cannot be unambiguously expressed by the conventional writing system. For example, the sentence in (31) (from Cruttenden, 1985) can convey either uncertainty about whether the speaker had been told or not, or indignation about the fact that he or she hadn't been told, but in the form in which it is presented here it is not possible to choose between those two interpretations:

(31) She might have told me.

In order not to give the misleading impression that features of intonation can be satisfactorily represented by the normal writing system, when I present examples of the oral reading that I recorded from the children in my study I shall use a modified version of the intonational transcription that I used. Sentences (32) and (33) illustrate the four key features of that transcription:

(32) As she' WATCHED | the °crowd grew in°creasingly ` RESTless | |
(33) As she °watched the' CROWD | she °grew in°creasingly ` RESTless | |

(i) The vertical bars demarcate the *tone units* (i.e. they show which words are pronounced together as a group), with the single bars indicating a sentence-internal boundary and the double bars a final boundary, of the kind that typically occurs at the end of a sentence when it is read aloud.
(ii) The capital letters reveal the *intonation nucleus* in each tone unit, i.e. the syllable which, by virtue of stress and pitch movement, is perceived as the most salient.
(iii) *Pitch movements* are shown by the symbols ' (for rising pitch) and ` (for falling pitch).
(iv) *Stressed syllables* (other than the nucleus, which is always stressed and doesn't need to be marked twice) are preceded by the symbol °.

Children's sensitivity to punctuation

Since in this transcription sentence-final boundaries are differentiated from sentence-internal boundaries by double bars, the transcripts revealed any places where the texts had sentence-final punctuation but where the children had not used appropriate sentence-final intonation. (As it happened, all but one of the transcribed extracts came from readings of books that had normal punctuation.) I was surprised to find how few such errors they made. From the earliest transcripts more than 90% of sentence boundaries were appropriately marked by intonation. Even when they were reading slowly and disfluently, word by painful word, with many errors, the children still recognised the end of a sentence when they reached it and signalled it prosodically, as in (34), which shows Sean at the age of 5;3 trying to read *went out in the dark*:

(34) (4) 'WENT | - 'TO | 'ONE | (3) 'IN (2) °the | (6) ` DARK | |
                  (Jennifer Yellow-hat Went Out in the Dark)

The numbers in brackets indicate the length of pauses in seconds, so clearly Sean was reading very slowly and hesitantly. The succession of one-word tone units, with each word apart from the last having a rising intonation, means that he was producing each word as if it was a separate item on a list. It doesn't seem possible that Sean was obtaining much meaning from this sentence or that he had a grasp of its underlying grammatical structure during his struggle to read it. And yet, he recognised the end of the sentence when he reached it, signalling it appropriately with a falling pitch on *dark*. There are many examples like this in the data. Quite often in the earliest sessions, when the children reached the end of a sentence they marked it not only with the right intonation but also with an audible sigh of relief. It seems reasonable to assume that they were, to some extent at least, being guided by the full stop and associated capital letter in their recognition of sentence boundaries. (It is likely that they were also guided to some extent by line ends, but this cannot be the sole explanation because, although sentences in the recorded texts often ended at line ends, there were many line ends that did **not** signal sentence ends and the children didn't show a marked tendency to give these a sentence-final falling intonation.) For this reason, I think it is a mistake for early reading books to exclude punctuation; beginning readers should have the benefit of as many clues as possible to the structure of what they are reading.

Misattribution of direct speech

A type of error that did occur fairly frequently was a mistaken interpretation of the relationship between a reporting clause and the adjacent direct speech. When there were several direct speech clauses within one stretch of text, an error could lead to a 'knock-on' effect, e.g.

(35) "My daddy won't let me keep
you," Costas said. "'Don't bring
stray cats here,' he will shout.
You are a stray cat, and that is
true." (*No More Pets*)

This passage is made particularly difficult by the direct speech of the father being enclosed within Costas's speech, and signalled (very subtly for a child) by single inverted commas inside the double ones. When Sean attempted this, at the age of 7, he mistakenly attached the first reporting clause, *Costas said*, to the following rather than the preceding utterance and was thus led into a further error with the attachment of *he will shout*, and a change of meaning:

(36a) My ` DADdy °won't l °let me ` KEEP

you | | - °Cos tas 'SAID | °don't °bring
°stray °cats ` HERE | | | He will 'SHOUT |
you °are a °stray ` CAT | and °that's
` TRUE | |

In other words, he read the passage as if it was punctuated like this:

(36b) "My Daddy won't let me keep you."
    Costas said, "Don't bring stray cats here."
    He will shout, "You are a stray cat and that's true."

In the longitudinal study, just over a quarter of the errors in the placement of final tone unit boundaries affected the relationship between reporting clauses and their associated direct speech. This high proportion suggested that the punctuation and layout were not giving children as much help as they needed. I wondered whether changes in layout to strengthen the effect of the punctuation might reduce the number of errors. Accordingly, I designed a small experiment to find out.

An experiment to assess the effect of layout on children's processing of direct speech

Materials

From the longitudinal study I selected three passages which had led to a number of speech attribution errors and I typed them out in two versions. The first (A) followed the layout of the originals precisely. In the second (B), as far as possible, reporting clauses were kept close to the direct speech that they referred to and separate from anything else. Example (35) above gives the original (A) version of the Costas extract; (37) shows what it looked like in the (B) version:

(37) "My daddy won't let me keep you,"
    Costas said.
    "'Don't bring stray cats here,' he will shout.
    You are a stray cat and that's true."

In this extract, there are two reporting clauses *Costas said* and *he will shout*. The alteration in layout affects the first reporting clause more markedly than the second: *Costas said* is now clearly separated from the following direct speech. The slighter difference for *he will shout* is that it is now on the same line as all the speech it reports.

In the three test passages there were 22 reporting clauses altogether. Of these, there were 12 where I judged that the layout of the original could be confusing and so made alterations for version (B) of the kind seen in (37) (None of the alterations was more extensive than those.) The remaining 10 reporting clauses were identical in layout in the two versions because a combination of printing conventions and accidents of spacing meant that the original was probably as good as it could be, e.g.

(38) "Let's go and see the elephants first," said
    Mrs Brown.
    "Oh good," said Jim, "I like elephants."

Subjects

The subjects were 40 children aged between 8;3 and 9;6 (with a mean age of 8;11) from two Year 4 classes in a school in a working-class area of Merseyside. They were tested on the Suffolk Reading test, which gave them reading ages between seven and ten. The children were divided into two groups of 20, matched by reading age. The mean reading age of both groups was 8; 7 (with standard deviations of 10.6 months and 10.1 months) — slightly below their mean chronological age.

Procedure

I tape-recorded the children from both groups in random order, as they read either the original layout or the altered version. I then listened to the tapes, without knowing which version a child had read, concentrating on the treatment of the reporting clauses. I recorded their reading on a standard sheet, which in every case had the reporting clause in the middle of a stretch of text. For example, the two reporting clauses in the Costas extract were set out like this on the standard sheet, regardless of which layout the child had seen:

(39a) "My daddy won't let me keep you," Costas said. "'Don't bring stray
    cats...
(39b) "'Don't bring stray cats here,' he will shout. You are a stray cat...'"

There were three possible types of error affecting the attribution of direct speech. These are illustrated in (40) to (43), with the mistaken reading set out beneath the punctuated version that appeared on the standard sheet. Only the double-bar boundaries are marked, as these were common to all the children who made that particular error; non-final boundaries, stress placement and choice of tune could vary from child to child without affecting the basic error.

One type of error was when a sentence-initial reporting clause was wrongly attached to the preceding sentence, e.g.

(40) Jane knew what it was. She said, "It's a deer."
    Jane knew what it was she said | | It's a deer | |

A possible consequence of this type of error was for the same stretch of speech to be attributed to two different speakers. This happened if an initial reporting clause was correctly attached to the following sentence and the next initial reporting clause was wrongly treated as if it was a final reporting clause and attached to the preceding sentence, e.g.

(41) Mrs Brown said, "Did you like the animals?" Jane said, "I liked the elephants but not the snakes."
Mrs Brown said did you like the animals Jane said I I I liked the elephants but not the snakes I I

Another type of error was when a sentence-final reporting clause was wrongly attached to the following sentence, e.g.

(42) "I fell down," the White Witch said. The queen looked at the broken broomstick.
I fell down I I The White Witch said the queen looked at the broken broomstick I I

A third type of error occurred when a reporting clause was not attached to the sentence on either side of it but was pronounced in isolation, e.g.

(43) "'Don't bring stray cats here,' he will shout. You are a stray cat and that's true."
Don't bring stray cats here I I He will shout I I You are a stray cat and that's true I I

I recorded the number of errors of the three kinds for each child. Only then did I enter on their record sheet which version they had read.

Findings

Altogether, there were mistakes on 14 of the 22 reporting clauses, with the number of mistakes per clause — out of a possible 40 — ranging from 1 to 30. Between them, the children made 102 mistakes, 67 by those in group A, who read the original layout, and 35 by group B, who read the altered layout. The average number of mistakes per child in group A was 3.35; in group B it was 1.75. The difference between these two results is highly significant ($p < 0.0005$), which suggests that even rather small changes of layout help to improve children's understanding of what they are reading.

The alterations to the layout in version (B) applied to 12 reporting clauses. The test passages also included 10 reporting clauses that were the same in both versions. Therefore, I compared the children's results on the 10 unaltered clauses with those on the 12 clauses that were presented differently in versions (A) and (B). Taking the error figures for all 40 children, there was a total of 12 errors on the 10 unaltered clauses (1.2 per clause) and 90 on the 12 clauses that had two versions (7.5 per clause). The distribution of the errors between the two groups is shown in Table 8.2.

Table 8.2 Number of errors per reporting clause in Groups (A) and (B)

Same layout in versions (A) and (B) (10 clauses — 12 errors)		Different layout in versions (A) and (B) (12 clauses — 90 errors)	
Group A (N = 20)	Group B (N = 20)	Group A (N = 20)	Group B (N = 20)
0.6	0.6	5.1	2.4

The table shows that, when there was no difference in layout, the performance by the two groups was the same, with 0.6 errors per clause each. This suggests that the groups were genuinely matched and that the difference in global score between them was not due to differences in reading ability but was a direct outcome of the altered layout. The table also shows that, when there were contrasting layouts, the difference between the two groups showed up even more clearly than on the overall error figures, because on this comparison there were more than twice as many errors by Group A (5.1) as by Group B (2.4). However, these results demonstrate that the altered layout did not remove all the difficulty, because the 12 altered clauses between them still produced four times as many mistakes per clause as the 10 unaltered clauses. This suggests that at least some of them contained some intrinsic difficulty which was exacerbated by the original layout of the direct speech.

Eight of the 22 reporting clauses were error-free and in seven of them I found something that at first surprised me. They are listed at (44):

(44) cried Costas
said the kitten
said Mrs Brown
said Jim
asked Mrs Brown
said Mrs Brown
said Mrs Brown

Obviously what they all have in common is the somewhat literary inverted verb–subject order, rather than the more prosaic subject–verb order. We have seen that the VS reporting clause can only occur **after** direct speech, not before it. This means that the grammatical structure makes the direction of attribution plain and removes the reader's dependence on the punctuation. As all of these VS reporting clauses were produced flawlessly,

I looked to see if there were any in the data that provoked errors. There were none. So this literary form seems peculiarly successful at enabling children to interpret direct speech correctly.

I said that this finding surprised me at first. That was because it has been so widely accepted that the language of early reading books should ideally be as close as is practical to the children's own spoken language, in order that they might bring their own linguistic expectations to bear on the interpretation of what they read. For example, the *Bullock Report* (DES, 1975) stated:

> A number of studies show that a printed text is easier to read the more closely its structures are related to those used by the reader in normal speech. (p. 92)

For this reason, some reading schemes (e.g. *Link-up*) deliberately use only the normal SV spoken form *the policeman said* in the early levels, eschewing the more literary VS form *said the policeman*. However, reporting clauses provide a clear instance of a difference between the spoken and the written forms of language, with the grammar of writing conveying a contrast that is expressed by features of intonation in speech. It seems to be the case that, far from hindering children, the literary construction actually helps them because it is more informative. While I was tape-recording the children reading in the experimental study, I noticed that they occasionally reversed the order of the elements in the reporting clauses. A check revealed that they never reversed the literary VS order to make it the prosaic SV. But there were nine occasions when the SV order was reversed to become VS.

Conclusions

The conclusions that can be drawn from the findings reported in this chapter relate firstly to the presentation of direct speech in children's reading books and secondly to practices that teachers might adopt in the classroom.

As far as reading books are concerned, it seems clear that the inclusion of reporting clauses and punctuation marks from the very beginning, far from making the young reader's task harder, actually provides helpful clues to what is going on. With regard to the choice of punctuation marks, double inverted commas have the following advantages over single ones: they are visually more salient; they can't be confused with apostrophes; and they are what children will be taught to use in their own writing. If the layout of the text allows reporting clauses to appear next to the reported speech, it is easier for children to attribute the words to the right characters. For this reason, very short line lengths can be unhelpful. When a reporting clause occurs **after** direct speech, it is less liable to be erroneously associated with the following words if it is presented in the inverted verb–subject form. For this reason, it is useful if final reporting clauses contain a noun rather than a pronoun, since with pronouns the verb–subject order is markedly literary.

As far as teaching practices are concerned, it is worth recognising that children are going to come across a number of different ways of presenting direct speech in their early reading books. (In fact, this diversity is greatest in the earliest stages — just when children are most sensitive to minor differences in typography; by the time they have a reading age of about seven, the books they read largely follow adult conventions of punctuation and so are relatively uniform.) Infant teachers (and those teaching children with reading difficulties) may find it useful to examine the books on their classroom shelves so that they have an idea of the various ways in which direct speech is presented. Armed with this information, they are in a position to point out similarities and contrasts to children if and when they judge it appropriate. They may also find that they develop a heightened awareness of some of the reading problems children have which stem directly from the punctuation and layout of direct speech. When they are making notes on children's oral reading, they may want to keep a record of the extent to which children are able to use punctuation to sort out speech attribution and so to derive meaning accurately from the text.

Although the diversity of the treatment of punctuation in early reading books may seem a nuisance, teachers can turn it to their advantage by encouraging children to explore the range of ways in which direct speech is presented. After all, if children are to gain the greatest benefit from features of punctuation, then it is helpful if they can become explicitly aware of them and of their functions (and names too). There are a number of activities — widely used in infant classrooms — which teachers can employ to heighten children's awareness of punctuation, to capitalise on the diversity of punctuation found within the class library, and to lead into children's own use of punctuation in their writing. For example, on photocopied pages of dialogue where the speech is unattributed children can write in the names of the speakers. On photocopies of well-punctuated dialogue they can use different coloured highlighter pens to demarcate the speech of different characters and can then choose speakers to read the parts aloud, like a play script. When they have books or comics where speech is presented in balloons, they can rewrite it as normal text, enclosing each character's speech in a set of inverted commas. When they have some independence as writers and begin writing their own stories containing dialogue, they can first of all write the words that are spoken in a different colour from the rest of the narrative and then enclose the coloured words in inverted commas. (There is an example of this use of colour in *The Shorty Books*.)

Teachers who are sensitive to the differences in the presentation of direct speech in the books in their classroom and who have derived a number of teaching activities from them are in a good position to equip children with strategies that will enable them to engage in the difficult task not only of decoding the individual words and sentences of their early reading books but also of responding appropriately to the punctuation, so that they can work out who says what.

9 Linguistics and the Logic of Non-standard Punctuation

ROZ IVANIC

Introduction

After spelling, punctuation is the feature which most frequently attracts comment from those who have a simple 'skills' view of what is involved in writing. Punctuation, like spelling, is seen as a matter of right or wrong. It is therefore easy to use as a criterion for grading and assumes great importance in an assessment-oriented education system. But this apparently simple skill eludes many borderline adult candidates in formal examinations in English Language in the UK. Why?

Unfortunately, many people seem to think that conventional punctuation has an inherent logic — much as many still think that the variety of English known as 'Standard English' is intrinsically more logical than other varieties. The parallel between the title of this article and Labov's famous article (1969) is intentional: the study I am reporting here contains evidence to suggest that unconventional punctuation is often a perfectly logical representation of ideas in writing, just as Labov showed that non-standard varieties of English are perfectly logical representations of ideas in speech. Another parallel is with spelling. Read (1986) has shown that children's 'creative' spellings are usually based on logical hypotheses about the relationship between sound and orthography; the evidence I have collected suggests that adults' 'creative' punctuation is also usually based on logical hypotheses about the relationship between sound, meaning and full stops.

Linguists who have studied punctuation have challenged the belief that there is an inherent logic in conventional punctuation — notice, for example, the sarcastic tone of Bolinger & Sears' words (which I have picked out in italics):

> Rhythm and intonation are roughly indicated by punctuation and capitalisation, but too much is left out and what remains suffers from a confusion of two aims: the representations of the breaks that we hear and the divisions that *logical-minded persons insist* that we write — the two usually agree, but not always. (Bolinger & Sears, 1981: 277)

However, examiners for formal English Language examinations seem to have no such doubts. In my experience standard sentence division has been used unquestioningly to distinguish between 'Pass' and 'Fail' categories in crucial gatekeeping examinations. If teachers want their students to get their qualifications, they have to be guided by the examiners, not the linguists.

Grammars and textbooks sometimes outline the conventions of punctuation; the most detailed I know is Appendix III of *The Comprehensive Grammar of the English Language* (Quirk, Greenbaum, Leech & Svartvik, 1985: 1609–39). This is a useful reference for those who already know the conventions, but I do not know of anyone who has learnt how to punctuate from this or any similar source. Others focus on the stylistic possibilities of punctuation, such as the clever use of commas for effect. Nash (1986), for example, describes 'Punctuation as a creative principle' (p. 100) in a whole chapter devoted to punctuation. In this he describes ways in which competent writers can choose between full stops, colons and semi-colons according to subtle shadings in the relationship between ideas, and how they can choose between structures requiring these full stop equivalents and structures requiring commas. The 'creative principle' approach is very attractive, provided you know to start with whether the choice you make will be judged as acceptable or not.

Neither employers nor examiners have any sympathy for unconventional punctuation. By 'unconventional' I don't mean 'idiosyncratic', I mean 'not obeying the conventions'. Idiosyncratic punctuation, as described for example by Nash, is often highly valued as a literary, creative quality of writing. Not obeying the conventions, however, is seen as sloppy, badly educated and illogical. As I have already suggested, most people do not question this judgement, and do not consider the fact that punctuation is, anyway, no more than a convention which has evolved over the years in a partly arbitrary way.

The convention which matters most to employers and examiners is the one of dividing sentences from each other with full stops. If students want jobs or the qualifications for further study, they must learn this convention. But what exactly do they have to learn? Perhaps all they have to do is to learn to mark off the sentences they say. This raises many questions. How do they know a sentence when they see — or hear — it? Are the 'sentences' they write the same as the 'sentences' they say? How can they learn what a sentence is? Is it a unit of sound, a unit of meaning, or a unit of syntax? It seems that learning to punctuate is inseparable from learning to write in sentences. Do students fail to punctuate or is their writing unpunctuable?

These are questions which can easily be overlooked by those who have themselves been successful in the education system, including politicians, leaders of commerce and industry, and teachers. By the time they qualify, most English teachers have acquired an intuitive sense of conventional sentence structure and sentence division. Those teachers who are able to explain the syntax usually choose not to — probably wisely: the linguistic terminology needed to explain, for example, that the first sentence of this paragraph has one main verb, would be confusing to say the least. Most teachers tend to provide rules-of-thumb for punctuation which can be divided into two broad categories:

Sound

Based on an idea about the relationship between intonation and punctuation, for example:

Read your writing aloud and listen for the pauses.

Put a full stop for a long pause and a comma for a little pause.

The punctuation marks on the written page take the place of the pauses, rise and fall of voice that we use when talking… If you have trouble with punctuation try using a tape recorder and record what you have written. Then play it back, and if you have read your written work properly, then you will be able to correct the incorrect punctuation… If you have trouble with dividing sentences, and often use a comma to divide them, instead of a full stop, this is a cure. (from a handout written by a senior examiner for 'O' Level English Language)

Meaning

Based on an idea about the relationship between meaning and punctuation, for example:

Break it up into chunks of meaning.

Put a full stop when you've come to the end of a complete idea.

Students follow this advice assiduously, yet they still make mistakes, particularly using a comma where conventional punctuation requires a full stop. As a teacher in Adult and Further Education this has always bothered me. I know intuitively that for many students this sort of advice does not work; it is not because they are stupid or lazy, so perhaps there is something wrong with the advice.

In this article I first summarise the questions other linguists have asked about learning to punctuate and the results of their research. I then present the results of my own study, in which I asked ten adult basic education students to explain their decisions about punctuating their own writing. I end with some implications for learning and teaching punctuation.

Other Studies of How Learner Writers Punctuate

Since punctuation is such a crucial part of learning to write, it is surprising that it has not received much attention from researchers (see Chapter 1 in this book). Some studies of the similarities and differences between spoken and written language (for overviews see Akinnaso, 1982, 1985) refer to punctuation, but only in general terms as a feature of written language with no direct counterpart in spoken language.

There are three studies which explore the implications of this for learning to write. Kress (1982) studied children learning to write and includes a chapter on 'the development of the concept of "sentence" in children's writing' (pp. 70–96). He points out that 'when children first learn to write they have to establish for themselves, gradually, what a sentence is all about' (p. 70). He illustrates this process with examples of children's writing from the age of six. He analyses the structure of the sentences, the sentence divisions and the corrections which children make to their own sentence structures. He shows how children progress from using sentences as textual or narrative units to manipulating the syntax of sentences to serve the needs of the larger structure of which they form a part.

Shaughnessy (1977) studied adults in basic writing classes in the City University of New York. She says:

> However unconventional a student's punctuation appears to be, it is worth studying for the insights it gives into his perception of sentence boundaries and of specific punctuation marks. (p. 17)

and

> ...the process whereby writers mark sentences is related to the process whereby they make them. (p. 28)

She gives illustrations of common confusions over punctuation from the work of students in Basic Writing classes. She explains what might be the logic behind the unconventional punctuation in each of her examples. She suggests that learner writers are using a simplified punctuation system, in which a full stop represents the end of an idea (not frequently reached), and a comma represents a link between ideas.

Danielewicz & Chafe (1985) made a detailed comparison of some samples of university people's speech and some samples of writing produced by students in a remedial freshman writing programme. They showed how:

> carrying over spoken prosodic habits into the punctuation of writing often leads to non-standard, and sometimes infelicitous results. (p. 224)

They identified seven prosodic characteristics of speech which can explain unconventional uses of punctuation in their written data. Their focus on prosody is an important contribution to our understanding of what is involved in learning to punctuate.

These three studies are extremely useful for writing teachers because they use linguistic insights to explain why learner writers often use unconventional punctuation. I approached the same issue from a different direction: I wanted to document student writers' own perceptions of what punctuation is for and what constitutes 'a sentence'.

Asking Learner Writers About Their Punctuation

The ten students who took part in this study were attending a 12-week, full-time course at Lancaster College of Adult Education. They were aged 19–27 and had no formal qualifications. Some reported interruptions to their schooling, but not all. Their aim was to brush up on basic skills in order to gain entry to vocational courses to train or retrain for various types of employment. For example, two were trying to gain places on secretarial courses; one was trying to get into the army; one had just left the navy and wanted to retrain for social work.

They had 'English' classes for nine hours a week, in three blocks of three hours. Most of the teaching was of an individualised, 'workshop' type, in which each student followed her/his own programme of work. Most of them worked on punctuation exercises from 'Punctuation Books One to Four' (Ledgard, 1977). The teacher said that the students did comparatively little free writing, but when they did she explained the punctuation in terms of meaning. She said: 'I use my hands a lot: the breaking up, the physical breaking up.'

These students were valuable sources of information for three reasons. Firstly, they were adults and therefore likely to be able to make more sophisticated observations on their own choices than children. Secondly, as developing writers they used a mixture of conventional and unconventional punctuation: I was interested in their explanations for both. Thirdly, they provided a section across many stages of development as writers, ranging from one who could not write independently at all to one who would be ready to take a formal exam in English ('O' Level GCE English at that time) within a few months.

I wanted to use a method which would integrate teaching, learning and research, in line with the principles of research and practice in adult literacy (see for example Ivanic & Simpson, 1988 and Hamilton, Ivanic & Barton, 1992). Briefly, these are:

(i)   learners should have a say in any research 'about' them;
(ii) learners' perspectives are essential to an understanding of their learning processes;
(iii) research is a means of learning: learners should benefit from any research which involves them;
(iv) research which interferes with normal practices can distort them; it is therefore essential to study learning as it really happens, not in an experimental environment.

I arranged to work individually with the students during English workshop time, so that they would not miss any regular classes or have to offer spare time for this work. I explained that it would amount to some extra individual attention, in which I hoped they would learn something about punctuation for themselves, as well as helping with the research.

My aim was to get as close as possible to the thought processes they used to decide where to put full stops in continuous composition, without interfering too much with the composing process itself. Following the example of, among others, Flower & Hayes (1980) and Odell, Goswami & Herrington (1983), I decided to ask each student individually to explain her/his reasons for punctuating as s/he did. However, I thought that doing this while writing would be too intrusive. I therefore decided to work with each student on approximately a page of a first draft of her/his own writing, as soon as possible after s/he had written it, discussing each punctuation mark s/he had used and other places which seemed relevant to me.

There seemed to me to be two important prerequisites for finding out how learner writers punctuate their own writing. One was that they should see some value and/or purpose in what they were writing. This seemed more important than that they should all be writing the same assignment. Secondly it was essential that the students should feel relaxed with me during the session in which we discussed their punctuation strategies. Instead of feeling anxious about whether they had made mistakes, I wanted them to see themselves as fellow researchers, exploring what's involved in punctuation along with me. I therefore decided to have a preliminary meeting with each student to establish a rapport, to discuss what they would be interested in writing and to help them with the initial planning of what they would write. At the end of this session they agreed to draft something without worrying too much about the punctuation, so that we could discuss it and work it out together in the second meeting. They also agreed to let me know when they had finished, so that I could arrange to discuss the punctuation as soon as possible after the initial drafting.

The meeting in which we discussed their drafts was very much like a one-to-one conference about writing-in-progress: the sort of discussion that is part of the 'process approach' to the teaching of writing. There were four differences. Firstly, we focused our discussion on punctuation and sentence structure in the context of the meaning and purpose of the writing, whereas in a tutorial we might have discussed a wider range of aspects of the writing. Secondly, we discussed every punctuation mark and potential place for a punctuation mark in the chosen section of the writing, whereas in a tutorial we would not have given such systematic and comprehensive attention to one aspect of the writing. Thirdly, we audio-recorded the discussion. Finally, we were uninterrupted and had no time constraints for the meeting: rare conditions for tutorials!

I asked questions like: 'Why did you choose to put a comma there?' I often probed further with one or more follow-up questions like, 'What would have been wrong with a full stop' or 'How did you know it was a sentence?' The students' answers to these questions and their general comments on writing and punctuation during the interviews are the primary data for this article.

It has often been argued that such mentalistic data does not necessarily reveal actual thought processes. (For a summary of this debate see Hayes & Flower 1983). It tells us only what the writers are able to articulate about what they *think* they did. Since it is impossible to know how learner writers actually make punctuation decisions, this data seems better than none at all. In spite of its limitations, I believe this is useful information to consider alongside what linguists have so far surmised from their own analyses of learner writers' finished work.

The Punctuation Strategies Used by Adult Learner Writers: An Overview

The students' writing was very varied: one dictated her piece to me; one wrote a total of 90 words; another wrote five pages. With those who had written more than a page we discussed first which part of their writing they would like to focus on, and selected approximately 150 words to discuss in detail. The number of punctuation marks and potential places for punctuation we discussed varied too, ranging from 11 in the shortest piece of writing to 40 in an extract from one of the longer pieces. I was not trying to make comparisons between the writers, so these differences didn't matter. What I was interested in was the sorts of explanations they gave for using or not using full stops and commas, which sorts of reasoning led to a correct choice of punctuation, and which did not.

I looked first at the ten pieces of writing, and identified how many correct and incorrect decisions the writers made about full stops and commas. Overall there were 150 punctuation decisions. Of these, 93 were places where there should have been a full stop. Fifty-seven were places where there should, or could, have been a comma. The distinction between 'should' and 'could' here is important. When I say 'should' I mean that the punctuation marks would be required by the examiners mentioned above. When I say 'could', the use of a comma is a matter of choice. With full stops (or full stop equivalents such as question marks) there were no complications: sentence division is deemed to be unequivocal, as discussed above. 'Full stop errors' include places where a comma was used when there should have been a full stop. Commas were more difficult to judge, as they are frequently optional. I always gave students the benefit of any doubt over commas, accepting the places they chose to put them as right if they were optional. However, if the choice of a comma in one place required the addition of another (see Quirk and others, 1985: 1615–19 and 1625–8), I registered it as an error. 'Comma errors' also include places where a full stop was used when there should, or could, have been a comma. Table 9.1 summarises the correct and incorrect decisions for commas and full stops. The fact that commas are often optional probably explains why there are fewer of them in the sample and fewer errors in these places. The 26% failure to identify the need for sentence division is what bars these writers from qualifications and jobs.

Table 9.1 Learner writers' correct and incorrect decisions about punctuation

	Correct	Incorrect	Total
Commas	46 (80%)	11 (20%)	57 (100%)
Full stops	69 (74%)	24 (26%)	93 (100%)
Total	115 (77%)	35 (23%)	150 (100%)

I then listened to the audio-recordings of the interviews to see whether I could identify any way of classifying the sorts of explanations the student-writers were giving for their punctuation decisions. It seemed to me that the students' explanations for choice of punctuation could be classified into four broad, and sometimes overlapping, categories:

Category	Example
Quantity	'I don't want three... I've got three commas in that lot.'
Sound	'You're going to have to have something there to tell you, OK, slow, don't stop but slow down.'
Meaning	'You've said about paddling in the lake and you're going on about the...now you're going to talk...well, write about...yeah, talk about the people sitting in the cars, which is sort of like stopping one thing and starting another.'
Structure	'It is not usual to start another sentence with "as well".'

Having identified these broad categories, I checked which were used for explaining the choice of commas, and which were used for explaining the choice of full stops. These figures are presented in Table 9.2.

Table 9.2 Learner writers' types of explanations for their punctuation decisions

Type of explanation	Quantity	Sound	Meaning	Structure	Total
Uses to explain decisions about commas	3 (5%)	8 (14%)	25 (44%)	21 (37%)	57 (100%)
Uses to explain decisions about full stops	7 (8%)	10 (11%)	59 (63%)	17 (18%)	93 (100%)
Total uses	10 (7%)	18 (12%)	84 (56%)	38 (25%)	150 (100%)

In Table 9.2 the percentages show how many of the total decisions in each row were justified by each of the types of explanation. It shows that these students explained their punctuation decisions in terms of meaning far more than any other way. In deciding where to use commas they mentioned structure almost as often, but in talking about full stops 'meaning' explanations (59) outnumbered all the others put together (34). This is not surprising since their teacher reported that she used and recommended this strategy too.

I then brought the information in Table 9.1 together with the information

Table 9.3 The frequency and effectiveness of four ways of explaining the need for a comma

Type of explanation	Quantity	Sound	Meaning	Structure	Total
Uses to explain correct commas	1 (33%)	7 (87%)	22 (88%)	16 (76%)	46
Uses to explain incorrect commas	2 (67%)	1 (13%)	3 (12%)	5 (24%)	11
Total uses to explain commas	3 (100%)	8 (100%)	25 (100%)	21 (100%)	57

Table 9.4 The frequency and effectiveness of four ways of explaining the need for a full stop

Type of explanation	Quantity	Sound	Meaning	Structure	Total
Uses to explain correct full stops	2 (28%)	5 (50%)	47 (80%)	15 (88%)	69 (74%)
Uses to explain incorrect full stops	5 (72%)	5 (50%)	12 (20%)	2 (12%)	24 (26%)
Total uses to explain full stops	7 (100%)	10 (100%)	59 (100%)	17 (100%)	93 (100%)

in Table 9.2, identifying which types of explanation were used for correct and for incorrect punctuation decisions. Tables 9.3 and 9.4 summarise this information. Table 9.3 contains the information relating to the use of commas, showing how often each type of explanation led to correct placing of commas, and how often each led to incorrect placing, or omission of commas. Table 9.4 contains the same information for full stops. In these tables, the percentages compare the correct with the incorrect uses to suggest the effectiveness of each type of explanation. For example, in Table 9.3, under the heading *Sound*, the figures show that, out of a total of eight explanations for commas in terms of sound, seven led to the correct placing of commas, that is 87%; whereas only one led to the incorrect placing of a comma, that is 13%. So explanations in terms of sound were associated with correct decisions far more than with incorrect decisions in this study, although it is, of course, impossible to generalise from such small numbers.

A comparison of Tables 9.3 and 9.4 shows that the most successful way of explaining the need for full stops is structure, whereas sound and meaning explanations are equally accurate for commas. The possible reasons for this are discussed in detail below. The numbers involved are not sufficient to be statistically significant, but they suggest a trend which might be worth further investigation. Sound and meaning undoubtedly emerge as unreliable criteria for sentence division for these students.

These tables provide a backdrop to the detailed discussion in the rest of this article of the exact wording of student-writers' explanations for their decisions, of particular examples of textual decisions and the way their writers explained them, and of which ways of thinking about punctuation lead to successful decisions and which do not. It is important to remember throughout that these are retrospective explanations for the decisions, not necessarily representing the on-line thought processes which the students used or would use while composing. It may well be that an explanation in terms of meaning, for example, is actually a fabricated rationale for a decision which was originally made on the grounds of a subconscious sense of structure. This is very likely in the case of many of the correct decisions: this, after all, is what many teachers are doing. Nevertheless, I think that this discussion of retrospective justifications throws some light on the actual process of punctuating. I deal with them under four section headings.

Quantity as a criterion for punctuating

This category includes explanations in terms of the number of punctuation marks used and the number of words written. Four of the ten students gave explanations of this sort and they appeared to be the least experienced writers. Learner writers probably grow out of thinking about punctuation in terms of quantity, realising that there are other more relevant criteria to consider. Certainly the reliability is abysmal: Tables 9.3 and 9.4 show that seven out of the ten explanations in terms of quantity were associated with incorrect decisions.

Some of these comments sounded naïve and slap-dash:

I thought it was about time I had a full stop.

However, before dismissing 'quantity' as an immature notion of what's involved in punctuation, it is worth considering in a bit more detail where the idea might come from. There may be a certain psychological reality to the idea that sentences do not go beyond a certain length — related, perhaps, to the number of morphemes that can be processed at one time in speech production and comprehension. Also, first encounters with written language may well give the impression that commas and full stops are distributed in fairly even numbers, that on average there are only one or two commas between full stops, and that sentences are about 22 words long. (Adult learners are particularly likely to get this impression, being protected, with any luck, from the unnatural structures of reading schemes.) In the absence of any other hypothesis, quantity must seem like a very reasonable guide to punctuation.

In addition, the students' comments show how misleading teachers' advice can be. If examination syllabi for English language say anything at all about evaluation criteria for written English, they usually include something about the superiority of 'complex sentence structure'. Here is what one of the writer's said about this:

> It's amazing because...I think the one thing that really gets you is you always seem to think that sentences should be...long things. You know, you're sort of like educated into that, that a sentence is a long string of words...and when you get little sentences you always tend to think you can't, no, you can't have a sentence...you never expect to have a sentence that short really, do you?

Sound as a criterion for punctuating

This category includes all explanations which refer to such things as 'stopping', 'pausing', 'a gap', 'a break', or 'a breather'. Tables 9.3 and 9.4 show that this criterion was used more often than 'quantity', but still only 18 times out of 150. Only five of the ten students used this criterion more than once. The most competent writer did not refer to sound at all in his explanations of punctuation. It appears on this limited evidence that developing writers discover that sound is not a reliable indicator of punctuation, and they eventually abandon it in favour of more effective criteria.

Example 9.1 illustrates the way in which a developing writer resorts to sound to justify his choice of punctuation.

Example 9.1

In spite of his unconventional spelling this student was a fluent writer: he wrote five pages about his work cutting the greens on a golf course. This extract occurs in the middle of his draft at the beginning of a new paragraph. The writer appeared to be totally engrossed in reliving his experience through writing at this point, so his punctuation probably reflects 'shaping at the point of utterance' (Britton, 1983) particularly closely. At Point 3 he is thirty words into the paragraph, but not at a point where syntax requires a full stop. He says:

> ...basically it had stopped. From there on I was taking a big breather to explain the next part now.

It seems that for him the spontaneous criterion was the completeness of the preceding structure; the fact that the words to come were not going to form an independent clause was not relevant. Competent writers hold their punctuation in abeyance at such points, but this learner writer did not. Sound and quantity seem to be bound up in each other here. It is as if the incorrect full stop is a surface sign that there is a limit to the amount of information he could hold in mind at one time. When he says 'it had stopped', he may well mean that he had come to the end of the quantity of information he could process. The 'big breather' is a bit of planning time in which he decides what to write next. These units of sound which the students report might be related to mental space, but punctuation has to reflect syntactic structuring.

Tables 9.3 and 9.4 show a remarkable difference in the reliability of sound for identifying where to put commas and full stops. Whereas explanations in terms of sound produced only 50% accuracy in decisions about full stops, it produced 87% accuracy in identifying where to put commas. It is interesting to speculate on the possible reasons for this difference. One explanation may be that commas are often optional. Writers can indeed use commas 'creatively', to emphasise the chunking of ideas within a sentence, or to increase suspense, as in this extract from one of the student's writing:

> I thought that I was going to be late for college, but I was horrifyingly mistaken.

Full stops, by contrast, are compulsory in particular syntactic environments, by the rules of conventional punctuation. Writers cannot omit or deploy them to enhance what they mean, unless they also adjust their syntax. When learners write two sentences on the same topic, they do not always expect their readers to pause between them: in their mind's ear they form a continuous stretch of meaning and sound. The implication seems to be that, contrary to expectations, reading what you have written, either out loud or to yourself, is not a fail-safe way of identifying the need for punctuation marks. The advice to 'put a comma for short pause' can be useful, but the advice to 'put a full stop for a longer pause' only works half the time, if that.

Two of the writers' comments suggest that individual styles of reading affect decisions about punctuation. This is how one student explained the choice of a comma which should have been a full stop:

> It was probably the way I was reading it. You know, I was probably reading it a bit fast and I thought, you know, just stick a comma there... I thought a comma would do, 'cos I was reading it out fast and I didn't think of stopping till I got to here.

Another student explained the use of an entirely optional comma:

> It's a place I would have naturally paused myself, I think, as I would read it, at the speed I would read it at any rate. I think that's more than enough of a mouthful for me to cope with at that point.

These comments suggest that learner writers who are using sound as a criterion for punctuating seem to be guided by the prosody they use when they read what they have written, either aloud or to themselves. Prosody is a notoriously elusive linguistic feature, and I cannot provide hard evidence in numerical terms here. However, in order to investigate this further I recorded one student reading her story out loud. This provides only one example, but I believe it is not unusual. She read from her first draft, before we had discussed the punctuation. Example 9.2 is an extract from her writing, with punctuation corrected in heavy pen.

Example 9.2

When she read it out loud, she did not use the intonation patterns normally associated with a full stop at Point 32. In fact, she seemed to be intentionally overriding the intonation conventions, as if to signal to the listener that meaning flowed from one sentence to the next. Her voice maintained a level tone, indicating that something was incomplete, and there was scarcely any perceptible break between the words 'rough' and 'it'. Her intonation seemed to indicate that what she was about to say would still be on the subject of the rough water. It is hardly surprising that she judged it inappropriate, by the criteria of both meaning and sound, to put a full stop at this point. By contrast, at Point 31 she took her time over the pause, perhaps confident that the rising tone on 'water' would be enough to carry the listener's attention forward to the specific details which follow.

I wanted to check whether this tendency to maintain intonation contours across full stops was unique to literacy students. I therefore listened to a variety of readers: parents reading to their children, university lecturers lecturing from prepared notes and news-readers reading from the auto-cue on television. This informal study suggests that all readers use intonation to chunk information into topic units above sentence level. This rules out the argument that literacy students have difficulty with punctuation because they are bad at reading out loud. In fact, they seem to make exactly the same use of intonation as professional readers do, from time to time maintaining a continuous flow of sound to signal continuity of topic, irrespective of syntax. They have learned a good deal more about reading out loud than their teachers give them credit for. These observations suggest to me that the advice to 'Put a full stop when you pause' can be quite misleading, and might be the culprit for quite a few missed full stops.

Meaning as a criterion for punctuating

This category included reference to such things as 'talking about', 'going on to say', 'starting something different', 'telling you about', 'another thought's coming to mind'. Tables 9.3 and 9.4 show that of the total 150 explanations over half (84) gave meaning as a criterion for placing punctuation marks, and of these 69 were correct. The popularity and relative success of the 'meaning' strategy must not be underestimated. Most new sentences really do start new topics or sub-topics. In this study the ten students marked all the clear boundaries between topics with full stops, both at the end of paragraphs and within paragraphs. When the topic boundary was fuzzy, however, as it often is, punctuation became much more difficult. For example, the writer of Example 9.3 found the semantic evidence confusing and used a full stop at Point 2 where there should, according to the elliptical syntax she used, have been a comma.

When I asked her why she'd chosen to use a full stop, she said:

Because I am not talking about 'why' — oh, I AM still talking about 'why' but now I change, I go on to it being a challenge. That bit (*the part from Point 2 to Point 3*) is more of a personal thing than that (*the part from Point 1 to Point 2*).

> I decied that I wanted to join the army because there are not many jobs in the area where I live;[1] then there are the advertisement in the paper and on the T.V.[2] Also the challenge that it would bring at all different levels from the M.P's to code translating.[3]

Example 9.3

Her analysis of what constitutes a change of meaning sufficient to warrant a full stop is very subtle, and very logical. This was true of nearly all the explanations students gave to justify their choice of full stops and commas in terms of meaning, correct and incorrect. The consensus seemed to be that the difference between full stops and commas is a matter of degree: the comma marks a weaker shift of meaning. Two comments on the correct use of a comma illustrate this:

because its going into slightly more depth.

like you're still on the same subject but you're going on to a different aspect of it.

Unfortunately, using meaning as the sole criterion for punctuating is misleading, since the end of an 'idea' is not always easy to identify, and does not necessarily correspond with the need for a full stop. The truth is, of course, that 'a different aspect of it' can sometimes be part of the same sentence, and sometimes begin a new one, depending on how you phrase it.

Learner writers paid attention to meaning more frequently in order to place full stops (59 times out of 93: 63%) than in order to place commas (25 times out of 57: 44%) (see Table 9.2). This may well be because the students have already realised that sound doesn't help much where full stops are concerned, although it does help with commas. From the evidence I collected, meaning appeared to be a more reliable criterion than sound for recognising where to put full stops, producing 80% as compared to 50% accuracy, but it was still letting too many errors slip through. Since students are recommended to punctuate according to considerations of meaning by this and many other teachers, it is disturbing to find that it leads them to miss one sentence division in five.

In this study, students used a comma or nothing in a place which required a full stop (or colon or semi-colon) 24 times altogether, and justified it in terms of meaning 12 times (see Table 9.4). In all 12 cases the students' judgements are supported by linguistic evidence: the relationship between the sentences is either explicitly marked by cohesive devices (as identified by Halliday & Hasan, 1976), or inferable from implicit coherence conditions. In four cases, the second sentence began with an anaphoric pronoun, particularly 'it', 'this', or 'they'. For example, in the following extract, the word 'this' makes the semantic link:

> The ADCO used to slide about when you went up the steep slope, this caused your lines to be squint and miss bits out.

In two cases, the second sentence began with a conjunction, as in this example:

> I decided I wanted to join the army because there are not many jobs in the area where I live, then there are the advertisements in the paper and on TV.

In five cases there was lexical cohesion between the two sentences. In the next example, there is both repetition of a word ('dog') and a semantic chain to do with being dead: 'not moving', 'blood running from throat':

> The dog was not moving, the blood was running from the dog's throat.

In five cases an implicit causal relation between the two sentences made them into a coherent unit, both for the writer and for readers, as in this example:

> It will be hard work in the army but I think I could put up with that, I am not afraid of discipline or being told what to do so that would not be a problem.

Cohesive links and coherence conditions are the linguistic devices for maintaining ideas across sentence boundaries. It is hardly surprising that students, using meaning as their criterion for placing full stops, omit them or use commas instead between sentences which are related in this way.

Some of the students' comments show just how seriously misled they are by the idea that punctuation is determined by meaning. When I told the writer of Example 9.1 that conventional punctuation required a full stop at Point 2, he said:

> It's carrying on: it's telling about the green. I've not changed dramatically. To say, like, to change it dramatically, to say: 'A man used to stand at the far edge of the green and pick his nose' or something, you see. It was carrying on from 'the green'... I could've swore blind it should've been a comma...it's come as quite a shock!

In addition, this extract illustrates the fact that it isn't always a straightforward question of correcting the punctuation. The cause and effect relationships in this short extract are in fact very complicated: the two levels cause the steep slope, and the steep slope in turn causes the green to be difficult to cut. Many teachers would put a wavy line between Point 2 and Point 4, suggesting that it needs rewording, rather than simply re-punctuating.

Examining these 12 places where students failed to identify the need for a full stop, I found something totally unpredicted. This particular error is far more common at the very beginning of a piece of writing than elsewhere. In this sample, seven out of the ten students missed their first full stop. It is interesting to speculate about the reasons for this. It may be that they plan some way ahead before they start writing. They are holding in mind a complex 'thought unit' as they first put pen to paper, and write comparatively fluently until that thought unit is exhausted. It appears that the first full stop represents the extent of their forward planning, and that this planning is of a semantic, not a syntactic nature. That is, they plan ideas rather than sentences. This would be in keeping with other work on the writing process which indicates that less skilled writers take a running jump into writing, then use previous text as a springboard for launching into the next 'sentence', rather than planning in a more global way (see, for example, Bereiter & Scardamalia, 1983; Jones, 1982).

There seems to be considerable evidence that students are aware of a change of grammatical subject. Of the 47 correct full stops which were justified by the criterion of meaning, 31 coincided with a change of grammatical subject. Several students' comments suggest that they were aware of the new grammatical subject as a sentence-starter. For example, the writer of Example 9.1 commented on his correct full stop at Point 4:

> Now I'm jumping on to the ADCO now, you see, going to be telling you about the ADCO, what the ADCO used to do, you see, because I've told you about the green. Now it's time, the turn of the ADCO.

Although explanations like this were given in terms of meaning, they reveal a sense of syntax. It seems as if the students don't have the metalanguage for explaining all the principles they are applying subconsciously. However, a few did manage to explain their punctuation in terms of sentence structure, as I discuss in the next section.

The relationship between sentence structure and punctuation

In this category I included all the comments which made reference to choice of wording. Table 9.2 shows that students did not mention structure often: only 38 of the 150 explanations fell in this category. This number is even less encouraging than it looks, because many were simply pointing out the need for commas in lists: this was a structural rule the students had learnt from their exercise books (Ledgard, 1977).

Some of the students were also able to explain the structural relationship between a main clause and a following relative clause. For example, in Example 9.4, this is how the writer explained the correct use of a comma at Point 18:

> and I think probably I'm starting with 'which'. 'which' is this (pointing to the word 'plants'). 'which' is backlogging.

Example 9.4

As Table 9.4 shows, structure was the most reliable criterion for sentence division: 88% of the decisions which students justified in terms of structure were correct. This could be explained by the fact that it was, on the whole, the more capable students who were able to explain their punctuation in terms of structure. There is perhaps a relationship between making correct punctuation decisions, general ability and/or educational development, and being able to give explanations in terms of structure. This contrasts with the observation I made when discussing explanations in terms of quantity, which seemed to be associated with lower general ability and/or educational development.

A particularly successful strategy was to use a combination of sound, meaning and structural criteria. The writer of Example 9.4 first read his draft aloud to himself slowly, then considered the relationship between two sections in terms of meaning and then checked it in terms of structure:

> ...and flower every year. Full stop. Well, it's going on to say something else again...going on to another explanation...probably because of 'this'? Does it make any difference? Is that sort of a hint that you should start a new sentence? Because of 'this'?

His attention to the way the word 'this' affected the punctuation indicated to me that he was using structure as his ultimate criterion.

It is interesting to consider how those students who could talk about sentence division in simple structural terms had learnt to do so. The writer of Example 9.4, the most able and ambitious writer of the ten, said:

> I'm probably thinking about when I'm reading books, and other people start new sentences, that probably appears and I tend to study it when I read it, how it's been punctuated — now I've started coming to this course. Probably before I never really, really bothered, you know. But I try to understand. When I read I try to understand it and see why they put the punctuation in where they put them in. You know, they're the professionals, like, aren't they, so, you know, you learn from them.

But he was probably exceptional in his determination to work out the 'logic', as he called it. Others can read a lot, acquire a sense of structure, but not be conscious of it. Another student who punctuated accurately reported that she liked reading. I asked her whether she thought that had helped her learn to punctuate. She said:

> No, because I don't look at the punctuation in the book, I just read the words, you know.

When I asked how she did learn, she said:

> You just get used to putting things in the right place.

This suggests that writers must learn to translate thoughts into written sentences, and thereby apply structural knowledge, but they don't necessarily have to be aware that they are doing so.

Conclusion: Implications for Teaching Punctuation

These adult learners' comments show that they are making a very good attempt to punctuate in accordance with phonetic and semantic patterns. Their decisions are often entirely logical by these linguistic criteria. Unfortunately, however, full stops do not always coincide with 'the end of a complete idea'. Intuitive judgments of what counts as a complete idea vary enormously, and shifts from one sub-topic to another can either be marked with a comma or a full stop, depending on the sentence structures. Translating mental processes into written sentences involves a great deal more than just putting full stops in pauses at the end of complete ideas. Sentences are to do with syntax. Sound and meaning can often be a guide to the syntax of written English, but only a guide. Beyond sound and meaning, learner writers face the uphill task of acquiring a subconscious sense of syntax for the places where punctuation doesn't correspond to their meaning units.

It seems that teachers' rules-of-thumb are potentially misleading. People who are imbued with written language assume that they can hear divisions which can, in fact, only be seen. But if I call into question teachers' stock-in-trade ways of advising learner writers on punctuation, then I ought to have something to offer in their place. This is not so easy. The main finding of this study was in fact that there are no simple solutions. However, there are some pointers to alternative practice which are worth mentioning.

Firstly, most learner writers are thinking about meaning while they are writing and not structure. Their punctuation is likely to reflect the way they want to chunk the content, irrespective of the internal wording they have used. This suggests that teachers might offer some alternative wordings to take account of the writer's preferred punctuation. This might sound a bit heretical, but students' meanings are surely more sacrosanct than students' words. Certainly there were times during this study when students chose to change a 'This' to a 'which' in order to preserve links between ideas.

Secondly, the evidence of this study, like Cohen & Hosenfeld's (1981), was that introspection about strategies seems to be a useful teaching method in itself. All the students felt that they were learning something from the research sessions. Of course individual conferencing of this sort is expensive on teacher-time, but occasional use of the technique may pay dividends.

Thirdly, each individual in this study used different strategies or combinations of strategies for punctuating. There are probably many ways of acquiring a sense of what a sentence is. Ideally teachers should be aware of the strategies each student is currently using so as to capitalise on the strengths and compensate for the limitations.

Fourthly, it is probably worth directing learners' attention to their wording as well as their meaning. Particularly, they may find it useful to know that 'It', 'This' and 'They' are often sentence-starting words. However, my experience is that this approach, like others, only helps some learner writers some of the time. Although a conscious awareness of structure proved to be the most reliable, there is no conclusive evidence that it is an essential prerequisite for accuracy.

Fifthly, while reading probably doesn't help students to learn to spell, it does seem to help some to punctuate. The quotations in the previous section show that reading can lead to either conscious or subconscious acquisition of a sense of sentence structure.

Above all, it is crucial for teachers to recognise that when students use non-standard punctuation it is not lazy or careless. This study has indicated that non-standard punctuation is frequently based on the prosody of reading aloud and on the information structure which underlies it. If we understand this, we will be in a better position to support students like this one in their struggle to shape meaning:

> You've got that many ideas rushing. You know what you want to say and then changing it into the words to put onto paper... 'cos speaking is completely different from writing so you...but I found it great.

Author's note

The insights in this article are not mine alone, but a co-production between me and the students at the Lancaster College of Adult Education. I would also like to thank David Barton for his invaluable help with the research project, and many other colleagues for their comments on earlier versions of the article. It is based on a paper first presented at the July 1987 BAAL (British Association for Applied Linguistics) Seminar on 'The Place of Linguistics in Applied Linguistics', and subsequently published as No. 51 in *Lancaster Papers in Linguistics*.

References

AKINNASO, N. 1982, On the differences between spoken and written language. *Language and Speech* 25, 97–125.
— 1985, On the similarities between spoken and written language. *Language and Speech* 28, 323–59.
ANON. 1978, *Punctuation Personified*. London: Scolar Press. (Originally published in 1824 by John Harris as one of a number of books in his 'Cabinet of Amusement and Instruction'.)
BACKSCHEIDER, P. 1972, Punctuation for the reader: A teaching approach. *The English Journal* 61, 874–77.
BAKER, C.D.and FREEBODY, P. 1989, *Children's First School Books*. Oxford: Blackwell.
BARTON, D. 1994, *Literacy: An Introduction to the Ecology of Written Language*. Oxford: Blackwell.
BENNETT, N. *et al.* 1984, *The Quality of Pupil Learning Experiences*. London: Lawrence Erlbaum Associates.
BEREITER, C. and SCARDAMALIA, M. 1983, Does learning to write have to be so difficult? In A. FREEDMAN, I. PRINGLE and J. YALDEN (eds) *Learning to Write: First Language, Second Language*. London: Longman.
BOLINGER, D and SEARS, D. 1981, *Aspects of Language* (3rd edn). New York: Harcourt, Brace and Jovanovitch.
BRITTON, J. 1983, Shaping at the point of utterance. In A. FREEDMAN, I. PRINGLE and J. YALDEN (eds) *Learning to Write: First Language, Second Language*. London: Longman.
BULLIONS, P. 1983, *The Principles of English Grammar*. New York: Scholar's Press. (Originally published 1846.)
CALKINS, Lucy M. 1980, When children want to punctuate: Basic skills belong in context. *Language Arts* 57, 567–73.
CALKINS, L. 1994, *The Art of Teaching Writing* (2nd edn). Portsmouth, NH: Heinemann.
CAREY, G. V. 1958, *Mind That Stop*. Harmondsworth: Penguin Books.
CAZDEN, C., CORDIERO, P. and GIACOBBE, M. 1985, Spontaneous and scientific concepts: Young children's learning of punctuation. In G. WELLS and J. NICHOLS (eds) *Language and Learning: An Interactional Perspective* (pp. 107–23). Brighton: Falmer Books.
CHURCH, F. 1967, Stress terminal patterns: Intonation clues to punctuation. *English Journal* 56 (3), 426–34.
CLAY, M. 1993, *Observation Survey of Early Literacy Achievement*. Portsmouth, NH: Heinemann.
COFFIN, T. 1951, Aids to the teaching of punctuation. *College English* 12, 216–19.

COHEN, A. and HOSENFELD, C. 1981, Some uses of mentalistic data in second language research. *Language Learning* 31, 85–313.

CORDEIRO, P. 1988, Children's punctuation: An analysis of errors in period placement. *Research in the Teaching of English* 22 (1), 62–74.

CORDIERO, P., GIACOBBE, M. and CAZDEN, C. 1983, Apostrophes, quotation marks, and periods: Learning punctuation in the first grade. *Language Arts* 60, 323–32.

CRUTTENDEN, A. 1985, Intonation comprehension in ten-year-olds. *Journal of Child Language* 12, 643–61.

DANIELEWICZ, J. and CHAFE, W. 1985, How 'normal' speaking leads to 'erroneous' punctuating. In S.W. FREEDMAN (ed.) *The Acquisition of Written Language: Response and Revision.* Norwood, NJ: Ablex Publishing Co.

DE GOES, C. and MARTLEW, M. 1983, Beginning to read and write: An exploratory study of young children's understanding of metalinguistic terms and graphic conventions. *First Language* 4, 121–30.

DENEAU, D. 1986, Pointing theory and some Victorian practices. *Year Book of Research in English and American Literature* 4, 97–134.

DEPARTMENT OF EDUCATION AND SCIENCE (DES) 1975, *A Language for Life.* London: HMSO.

— 1989, *English in the National Curriculum.* London: HMSO.

DEPARTMENT FOR EDUCATION (DfE) 1993, *English for Ages 5–16 (1993).* London: HMSO.

— 1995, *English in the National Curriculum.* London: HMSO.

DICKSON, W.B. 1900, *Modern Punctuation.* New York: Putnam and Sons.

DONALDSON, M. 1978, *Children's Minds.* London: Fontana Books.

DOWNING, J. 1970, Children's concepts of language in learning to read. *Educational Research* 12, 106–12.

— 1976, The reading instruction register. *Language Arts* 53, 762–6.

ECKHOFF, B. 1986, How basal reading texts affect children's writing. Paper presented at 67th Conference of American Research Association, San Francisco.

EDELSKY, C. 1983, Segmentation and punctuation: Developmental data from young writers in a bilingual program. *Research in the Teaching of English* 17 (2), 135–56.

EDELSKY, C., ALTWERGER, B. and FLORES, B. 1991, *Whole Language: What's the Difference?* Portsmouth, NH: Heinemann.

FERREIRO, E. and TEBEROSKY, A. 1984, *Literacy Before Schooling.* London: Heinemann Educational Books.

— 1991, La construcciùn de la escritura en el niño. *Lectura y Vida* 12 (3), 5–74.

FLOWER, L. and HAYES, J. 1980, Identifying the organisation of writing processes. In L.W. GREGG and E.R. STEINBERG (eds) *Cognitive Processes in Writing.* Hillsdale, NJ: Lawrence Erlbaum.

FREEDMAN, A., PRINGLE, A. and YALDEN, J. (eds) 1983, *Learning to Write: First Language, Second Language.* London: Longman.

FURNESS, E. 1960, Pupils, pedagogues and punctuation. *Elementary English* 37, 184–9.

GEE, R. and McCLELLAND, P. 1992, *Punctuation Puzzles.* London: Usborne Books.

GENTRY, L. 1981, Punctuation instruction in elementary school textbooks. *ERIC Document ED 199 757.*

GOODMAN, K. 1993, *Phonics Phacts.* Portsmouth, NH: Heinemann.

— 1994, Reading, writing, and written texts: A transactional sociopsycholinguistic view. In R.B. RUDDELL, M.R. RUDDELL and H. SINGER (eds) *Theoretical Models and Processes of Reading* (4th edn). Newark, DE: International Reading Association.

GOODMAN, Y. 1979, Letters. *Language Arts* 56 (5), 482.

— 1980, The roots of literacy. In M.P. DOUGLASS (ed.) *Reading: A Humanising Experience.* Claremont: Claremont Graduate School.

GRAVES, D. 1983, *Writing: Teachers and Children and Work.* Portsmouth, NH: Heinemann.

HALLIDAY M.A.K. and HASAN, R. 1976, *Cohesion in English.* London: Longman.

HAMILTON, M., IVANIC, R. and BARTON, D. 1992, Knowing where we are: Participatory research in adult literacy. In J.P. HAUTECOEUR (ed.) *ALPHA92: Current Research in Literacy: Literacy Strategies in the Community Movement.* Hamburg: UNESCO Institute of Education.

HAYES, J. and FLOWER, L 1983, Uncovering cognitive processes in writing: An introduction to protocol analysis. In P. MOSENTHAL, L. TAMOR and S.A. WALMSLEY (eds) *Research on Writing: Principles and Methods.* New York: Longman.

HILL, K. 1984, *The Writing Process.* Nelson (Australia).

HONAN, P. 1960, 18th and 19th century punctuation theory. *English Studies* 41, 92–102.

IVANIC, R. 1988, Linguistics and the logic of non-standard punctuation. *Lancaster Paper in Education No 51.* Department of Linguistics and Modern English Usage, Lancaster University.

IVANIC, R. and SIMPSON, J. 1988, Clearing away the debris: Learning and researching academic writing. *Research and Practice in Adult Literacy Bulletin No. 6,* 6–7.

JONES, S. 1982, Attention to rhetorical information while composing in a second language. In C. Campbell (ed.) *Proceedings of the 4th Los Angeles Second Language Research Forum.* Los Angeles: University of California.

KRESS, G. 1982, *Learning To Write.* London: Routledge and Kegan Paul.

LABOV, W. 1969, The logic of non-standard English. *Georgetown Monographs on Language and Linguistics* 22, 1–43.

LEDGARD, T.G. 1977, *Punctuation Books: One to Four.* London: Cassell.

LITTLE, G. 1984, Punctuation. In M. MORAN and R. LUNSFORD (eds) *Research in Composition and Rhetoric.* Connecticut: Greenwood Press.

LOVELL, A. 1907, *Punctuation as a Means of Expression: Its Theory and Practice.* London: Sir Isaac Pitman and Sons.

McCORKLE, J. 1962, Eliminating the guess work from sentence punctuation. *The English Journal* 15, 673–80.

McDERMOTT, J. 1990, *Punctuation For Now.* London: Macmillan.

MICHEL, P. 1994, *The Child's View of Reading.* Mass: Allyn and Bacon.

MILLIGAN, J. 1941, Learning about punctuation in the primary grades. *Elementary English Review* 8, 96–8.

MOE, M. 1913, Teaching the use of the comma. *The English Journal* 2, 104–8.

MOON, C. 1994, *Individualised Reading.* Reading: Reading and Language Information Centre, University of Reading.

NASH, W. 1986, *English Usage: A Guide to First Principles.* London: Routledge and Kegan Paul.

NATIONAL WRITING PROJECT 1990, *Perceptions of Writing*. London: Thomas Nelson.

NOBLE, T. 1984, *The Day Jimmy's Boa Ate the Wash*. New York: Dial Books.

NUNBERG, G. 1990, *The Linguistics of Punctuation*. California: Center for the Study of Language and Information.

O'CONNOR, J.D. and ARNOLD, G.F. 1973, *Intonation of Colloquial English*. London: Longman.

ODELL, L., GOSWAMI, D. and HERRINGTON, A. 1983, The discourse-based interview: A procedure for exploring the tacit knowledge of writers in non-academic settings. In P. MOSENTHAL, L. TAMOR and S.A. WALMSLEY (eds) *Research on Writing: Principles and Methods*. New York: Longman.

PARKES, M.B. 1992, *Pause and Effect: An Introduction to the History of Punctuation in the West*. London: Scolar Press.

PARSONS, E. 1915, Bowing down before the God of punctuation. *English Journal* 4, 598–9.

PARTRIDGE, E. 1977, *You Have A Point There*. London: Routledge and Kegan Paul.

PERERA, K. 1985, 'Do your corrections properly': How children can improve their writing. *Child Language Teaching and Therapy* 1.

— 1989, The development of prosodic features in children's oral reading. PhD thesis, University of Manchester.

PFLAUM, S. 1986, *The Development of Language and Literacy in Young Children*. Merrill.

PIAGET, J. 1970, Piaget's theory. In P.H. MUSSEN (ed.) *Carmichaels's Manual of Child Psychology*. New York: John Wiley and Sons.

PRESSY, S.L. and CAMPBELL, P. 1933, The cause of children's errors in capitalisation. *English Journal* 22, 197–201.

QUIRK, R., GREENBAUM, G., LEECH, G. and SVARTVIC, J. 1985, *A Comprehensive Grammar of the English Language*. London: Longman.

RABAN, B. 1986, Children's thinking about reading and writing. *Occasional Paper No 1*, Reading and Language Centre, University of Reading.

READ, C. 1970, Pre-school children's knowledge of English phonology. *Harvard Educational Review* 41 (1), 1–34.

— 1986, Creative spelling by young children. In T. SHOPEN and J.M. WILLIAMS (eds) *Standards and Dialects in English*. Cambridge, MA: Winthrop.

REID, J. 1966, Learning to think about reading. *Educational Research* 9, 56–62.

— 1983, Into print: Reading and language growth. In M. DONALDSON, R. GRIEVE and C. PRATT (eds) *Early Childhood Development and Education*. Oxford: Basil Blackwell.

ROTTENBERG, C. 1992, Becoming literate in a preschool class: Literacy development of hearing-impaired children. *Journal of Reading Behavior* 24 (4), 463–79.

ROURKE, C. M. 1915, The rationale of punctuation. *Educational Review* 50, 246–58.

RUIZ, N.T. (in preparation) A young deaf child learns to read: Implications for literacy development.

— (in press) A young deaf child learns to write: Implications for literacy development. *The Reading Teacher*.

SALISBURY, R. 1939, The psychology of punctuation. *The English Journal* 28, 794–806.

— 1945, The reading road to punctuation skill. *Elementary English Review* 22, 117–23 (and 138).

SHAUGHNESSY, M. 1977, *Errors and Expectations.* New York: Oxford University Press.

SHOPEN, T. and WILLIAMS, J.M. (eds) *Standards and Dialects in English.* Cambridge, MA: Winthrop.

SMITH, F. 1982, *Writing and the Writer. New Hampshire: Heinemann.*

SMITH, F. 1992, Learning to read: The never-ending debate. *Phi-Delta-Kappen* 73 (6), 432–35.

SOPHER, H. 1977, The problem of punctuation. *English Language Teacher's Journal* 31 (4), 304–13.

SULZBY, E. 1992, Transitions from emergent to conventional writing. *Language Arts* 69 (4), 290–7.

SYMONDS, P. and LEE, B. 1929, Studies in the learning of English expression, No 1: Punctuation. *Teachers College Record* 30, 461–80.

THORNDIKE, E. 1948, Punctuation. *Teachers College Record* 49, 531–7.

WERNER, H. 1978, The concept of development from a comparative and organismic point of view. In S. BARTEN and M. FRANKLIN (eds) *Development Processes: Heinz Werner's Selected Writings.* New York: International Universities Press.

WILDE, S. 1987, An analysis of the development of spelling and punctuation in selected third and fourth grade children. Doctoral dissertation, University of Arizona. *Dissertation Abstracts International* 47, 2452A.

— 1988, Learning to spell and punctuate: A study of eight and nine year old children. *Language and Education* 2 (1), 35–59.

— 1992, *You kan red this! Spelling and Punctuation for Whole Language Classrooms, K-6.* Portsmouth, NH: Heinemann.

WILLIAMS, C.L. 1991, The verbal language worlds and early childhood literacy development of three profoundly deaf preschool children. Doctoral Dissertation, The Ohio State University.

WILKINS, J. 1668, *An Essay Towards a Real Character and a Philosophical Language.* London.

WILSON, J. 1844, *A Treatise on Grammatical Punctuation.* Manchester.